# It Only Takes One Look

Bob Gushwa

River Birch Press
Daphne, Alabama

*It Only Takes One Look*
by Bob Gushwa
Copyright ©2021 Bob Gushwa
All rights reserved. This book is protected under the copyright laws of the United States of America. This book may not be copied or reprinted for commercial gain or profit.

All Scripture quotations, unless otherwise indicated, are taken from the Holy Bible, New International Version® NIV®. Copyright ©1973, 1978, 1984 by International Bible Society. Used by permission of Zondervan. All rights reserved.

Scripture marked ESV is taken from the ESV® Bible (The Holy Bible, English Standard Version®), copyright ©2001 by Crossway, a publishing ministry of Good News Publishers. Used by permission. All rights reserved.

ISBN 978-1-951561-52-9
For Worldwide Distribution
Printed in the U.S.A

                    River Birch Press
                      P.O. Box 868
                    Daphne, AL 36526

# CONTENTS

Preface   *v*

Introduction   *vii*

One: Innocent Beginnings   *1*

Two: Choices   *12*

Three: Ninth and Tenth Grades   *23*

Four: Junior Year at Riley   *34*

Five: Senior Year   *41*

Six: Life in the Military   *59*

Seven: Kaiserslautern, Germany   *71*

Eight: Fort Detrick, Maryland   *84*

Nine: Vicenza, Italy   *93*

Ten: Fort Carson, Colorado   *102*

Eleven: Innocence Lost   *108*

Twelve: How Long, Lord?   *133*

Thirteen: Death of a Son   *162*

Fourteen: Probation and Treatment   *173*

Fifteen: Counting the Cost of Pornography   *193*

Sixteen: The World in Need of Hope   *221*

Seventeen: Conclusion   *232*

# Preface

There is a problem in this country, and around the world. Many say that it is normal. Many say that pornography doesn't concern them or doesn't intrude on their personal life.

Maybe so, but it still does intrude when you're watching television, driving, or sneaking a peek at billboards. Maybe there's not nudity, but Hollywood is coming close to it.

Pornography is nothing to play with. It always starts out with a look, and most likely you won't put it down. Why not? What is it about these pictures and stories that keep you coming back?

Hollywood, pornography, adult clubs, and prostitution all have one thing in common—they entice you to keep coming back for more. They work on the sexual desires of mostly men.

In this book is a true story of a boy who innocently picked up a magazine on his way to school. I share with you what happens when you give in to these desires. It began in 1964. As the industry grew, so did the boy. His mind was subject to acting out what he was taught from numerous magazines.

He lived with a lifetime of failures. When he became an adult and made this one mistake, he was told there was no hope for him. He would always be that way. Was he?

# Introduction

At the age of fourteen, this young boy didn't know what was waiting for him on that bright and shiny day while walking to school. He didn't know his life would be turned upside down. Many trials, temptations, and failures lay ahead. But who knew?

His downfall began on his way to school and ended in a church with a dead body lying in a casket before him. What he dreamed about having, he gave up for the pleasure of pornography. Time after time he was given the opportunity to surrender this habit before it got out of control.

He started with just an innocent peek, but as time went by that peek became a habit, which eventually became an addiction. He should have listened early on to the voice that was telling him to put it down. But he didn't know how bad the outcome would be. He couldn't stop thinking of the feeling he had when he saw the pictures. It took him forty-four years living in the sin of immorality to surrender that addiction to the Lord.

What is it about sex offenders that makes so many of them turn to pornography? What makes fornication and adultery so dangerous? Why does God allow people to make decisions that hurt other people, especially children?

I have been questioned so many times about my life: "You had it so good with your first marriage. How could you destroy that?" "When you were convicted, why couldn't you see how bad it was and stop?" "Did you truly want God to take away your habit?" "God saw your pain and what it was doing to your marriage. Why didn't he intervene?"

I have experienced the dark world of pornography that leads to immorality—the losses, the tears, the fears I felt knowing I would face consequences if I gave in.

Should a believer in Christ give in to pornography? Should a believer cheat on his wife? Ask yourself: Have you ever trusted in the Lord to forgive you of all your sins? The Christian knows the answer, and the Christian knows sin entails consequences.

The deeper you sink, the less you care about your sins. Then your depravity keeps getting worse until the Lord puts up a wall. Then you must decide to either listen and obey, or to be put on a shelf for no use to God.

I never wanted to believe that God would put me on a shelf until the day came. God's patience had run out. But why me? Why had God always had this special plan for my life? Why had he allowed this to happen?

"Here I am, now older, Lord. How can I be of service for you at this age?" I eventually realized why he had this plan for me.

Pornography became more popular in the midsixties. Yes, it had been around before that but was not as explicit before then. Pornography affects our everyday lives. It affects our thoughts and minds. God allowed me to live through it, but I didn't understand why at the time.

He knew all along that I would eventually be willing to speak out against it. He knew that child pornography would become a growing industry. He knew the fire that would be lit by these wicked men who pay top prices for soliciting pornography. To understand this, I had to walk through it.

I kept questioning why God would allow me, or any other Christian, to live that life, especially after I kept repenting of my sin. At the age of fourteen, who knew the plan God had for me?

As I went through those perilous times, God kept my spiritual beliefs ever present. Though I was disobeying him, I was learning how wicked and addictive this sin was. I now know what it can do. I know the power that overwhelms men and even women. I know the pain of trying to fight this, only to go back into it deeper every time.

Most sexual activities are kept in secret. Why is that? If the porn industry is so normal and widespread, then why keep it a secret?

I kept my pornography a secret from 1964 to 2007. No one knew I had such a bad issue with it because I was protecting my family. Nobody was going to take them from me, but someone did, in October 2007. That ended pornography for me but not the war of thoughts. My thoughts continually tempted me to go back into that dark world.

So, here is my story of the battle that raged within my mind—the battle with the devil, the pleading with the Lord. Suicide almost became my answer. I took the life of an unborn baby and paid the price with another life.

This story tells how committed God is in forgiving the sexual sins of those who will trust in him. You will find by reading this story that God will forgive any sin, no matter how deep you have dug a hole. He has this unbelievable love for his creation. But I have learned that God's love does not tolerate disobedience.

Though God is all-knowing and sees our future, we don't. So we are given free will to choose. Though God allowed me to go through this experience and would not take it away, I was still responsible for my mistakes and disobedience. I paid a high price for them, but when I view the whole picture of who Jesus Christ is, I can understand it.

This story was not about me. It has always been about God. To whom did I run? To whom did I cry out?

This story begins with me taking only one look, and I was hooked. What a life it has been. What a redeeming God I have! Never did he let go and leave me behind. That is what this book is about. The Lord will always have the last word, but only if you will obey him.

## One

# Innocent Beginnings

You never would think a little boy in the third grade could get his heart broken by a girl. But it happened to me on a church hayride in late October of that year. I liked this little girl, but all I wanted to do was kiss her on the cheek. I was teasing her, as little boys like to do, by throwing hay on her.

She smiled and turned away each time a little hay landed on her lap. As I moved to sit next to her, another boy moved in. Bruised by the missed opportunity, which I instantly perceived as rejection, I returned to my lonely seat and kept my hurt to myself. *How could this be? She smiled at me. I thought she liked me.*

I hopped out of the wagon and walked behind the two of them as our church hayride was ending. I couldn't imagine why she chose that kid over me. Never had I experienced this kind of hurt. I was rejected. *Who was this stupid kid anyway? No mind, he can have her. I'll just hang out with the guys.*

My brother and sisters used to reminisce about the small house we grew up in with fruit trees, chickens, a pig, and an acre of growing vegetables. I spent many days there hanging out, climbing a cherry tree and eating cherries until my stomach ached. Oh, how I hated those chickens and those two mean geese, but I loved to get them all riled up until they hissed and chased me.

My brother and I were the ones left plucking and cleaning the chicken after my uncles killed them for supper. I remember getting a kick out of the cats jumping out of the way, unsettled by the flipping chickens.

Those days were simple. We enjoyed family reunions, church potlucks, and summer camps. During this time, some of my most fond memories included the incomparable, special love I received from my grandparents.

Yes, those days have long gone. Now a Thanksgiving dinner features bickering at the table. Christmas includes fighting over who got the best gift, and family reunions can hardly be scheduled anymore because we can't get along enough to enjoy one another's company.

Sure, bickering, fighting, and jealousy have always tried to plague the family, settling in every so often but only in isolated, harmless instances. The information age has brought this world many new opportunities. Unfortunately, it has also oozed into the hearts of families, overcoming reason and compassion, often testing limits, and breaking rules that didn't suit plans.

My bad choices began before I delved into the world of pornography. One day, on the way to school, I decided to steal some pencils and a candy bar from the local grocery store. The assistant manager tried to chase me all the way to school, but I was too fast and clever, hiding behind a group of uncut bushes. Since he was not able to get a glimpse of me, I never got caught. I decided to take my chances with another bad choice at a store down the street from the one I had stolen from weeks earlier. This store welcomed me inside as the quiet chime announced my entrance through the automatic doors.

"Do you have any empty boxes," I asked. "We're moving, and my mom asked me to come down here."

As he turned toward the storage closet behind him, I stole some snacks, which I hid inside the empty boxes he handed me. Out I walked with stolen goods. My friends and I hid in a field and ate the snacks.

Other parts of my early life bring back good thoughts. Memories of my mom and my grandmothers canning fruits and vegetables are sweet but still make me sweat. All the love and effort they put into the activity was worth it. Family gatherings, barbeques, cousin time—life was great back then, but from as early as I can remember, I could always sense this emptiness.

I spent most of my life trying to fill the emptiness with whatever I thought could satisfy me. I was determined to figure out a way. I hated to move from that little farm, but eventually we moved to a small community called River Park. It was here where I discovered pornography.

Back in junior high, I had not been educated as today's young teenagers are in public school about the feelings I had been experiencing since I went on that hayride. Without sex education at school or home, how was I to learn? In fifth grade, I convinced some girls to play nurse and doctor a few times, but I did not understand my mood swings nor the onset of puberty.

I never liked going to school to learn, but I did like seeing the girls in their miniskirts. I had no idea what evil was taking root in my life. I just followed whatever I chose to bring me pleasure to fill an emptiness I could not identify.

## Trash in the Alley

I can remember as if it were today: Snow covered the ground from a quick-moving storm two days earlier. I loved walking in the snow, so this brisk, clear morning I dressed in a smile, knowing at least I would have a fun walk to school.

Little did I know, that would be the day my eyes would lead me into a steady decline that would traverse over the next forty-four years. Although this alley had become a most familiar path between home and school, on this day something unusual would catch my eyes.

*What is this?* I thought as I stepped closer. Seeing that it was a magazine, it didn't occur to me that a darkness lay in wait beneath the glossy cover. Bending over to pick it up, I felt a sudden snap inside me, like a brick dropping on my heart. In an instant, my mind absorbed the shock, and my body warmed and fluttered at what my eyes beheld. Nobody had to tell me what it was, nor did they need to. I liked it. What I was feeling in that alley took me to another place. I had never seen anything like this. I had wondered but never thought I would see it here in this alley.

*Why am I feeling like this? What is going on with my body. These feelings? I like them, but I feel like I shouldn't. I think I'll keep this magazine until I figure this out. Nobody needs to know, especially my mom. Yeah, I won't tell my mom.*

Knowing I had to get to school before the bell rang, I turned and continued walking slowly enough that I could turn the pages of my new mystery, viewing more pictures. I had never turned the pages of a book slower than this magazine. I was taking more time to examine and internalize the pictures I was viewing.

Eventually, I shared the magazine with my friends,

sparking a whole lot of questions that I didn't really want answers to. I only knew that I had found something life changing in the alley. I would never be the same again.

## Early Days in the Church

Every year when I was young, our church had a youth rally, an enjoyable event where I felt accepted. I used to love it when they turned the bright lights down just before the preaching. The big cross on the ceiling turned to different colors. The atmosphere felt cozy, like a living room full of friends. The music was great, and the preaching spoke to my heart.

One year, before the main service started, a visiting pastor and his wife met with the boys and girls in separate rooms. I can remember to this day the words he spoke. He said: "If you give in to sexual temptations before marriage, you will regret it the rest of your lives."

In the back of my mind I was listening but also trying to ignore what he was saying. *I have one thing you don't have: naked pictures of females. How would you know what I am going through? You are not going through what I am. I can look at them anytime I want to.* As he was talking, I kept making excuses in my mind: *You mean the feelings I get every time I see those nasty pictures in my magazine? So why do I have them? Why are they so bad when it feels so good when I see them and think about the girls in them?*

I kept my thoughts to myself, though, because I would have been too embarrassed to speak them aloud. After our main service, we were all invited to accept Christ as our personal Savior. Our church always gave altar calls. I had always thought these were for bad adults, not for good, curious boys like me.

The preacher pointed to this big window that looked down the corridor where the front doors were and said, "There is no guarantee that you will come back next week. If you die lost, where will you go? Heaven or hell?"

*Whoa. Now he's talking about dying. How did he go from desires to regret, then to hell?*

I knew about Jesus. I knew he died on the cross and rose again on the third day. Sure, every Good Friday our church showed the movie *The Greatest Story Ever Told*, and I watched. Sure, I had come to realize that meditating on the magazines was bad, but going to hell over them? Wasn't that a bit extreme?

Sitting on the pew a few moments longer, I convinced myself that because I knew something wasn't right about what I was doing that I needed to change somehow. The feelings of warmth and excitement the magazines gave me began to make way for other, less pleasing feelings of guilt.

So, by faith, I walked down the aisle and gave my life to Christ. I had made a change and I expected my life to follow suit. I didn't know that being a Christian was a process that would last my whole life. However, not until much later in life would I realize there was more to this faith in Jesus Christ.

As a young boy, walking down an aisle to rid himself of guilt over dirty magazines, I knew nothing of what it would take to overcome the bondage of pornography until decades later. I knew nothing of the Holy Spirit, God, or deity. What I did know as a young boy was that emptiness inside. I thought at the time that when I got off my knees, I would be a Christian.

"Great. I did it. Now what?"

Innocent Beginnings

## House Games

While living in the River Park Community during junior high school, a cute girl lived across the street from me. I was shy around girls, but she and I became interested in each other. She would stare at me; I would stare at her. One thing led to another, and this girl and I became boyfriend and girlfriend. Even though I had converted to Christ at the youth event, I still succumbed to the temptations of the nasty magazine pictures.

Now that I had a real-life girlfriend, my desires for the pictures developed into a desire to see my girlfriend nude. I knew I would have to trick her, though, because I was afraid to ask her. Somehow, I convinced her to play the role of my wife.

When my parents were gone, she came over, and we would lie on my bed. We would start with just talking, but our activities soon escalated from talking to kissing. Our playing house would end abruptly when my mother caught us in bed one day. Of course, my mom then told my girlfriend's mom. My family moved two miles away to get some distance between us.

Living two miles away made it less convenient to play house with my her. But I still walked to meet her, and then the two of us would hang out at the local drug store fountain counter. Those were the days I like to remember—sipping a soda together, laughing at each other's jokes, blushing at each other's sweet words, and watching people swing open the doors with kids in tow.

But still, one thing would lead to another, and our continued activity of playing house convinced her parents to move farther away. Some things I held inside, never to tell my parents. How they knew I had a problem, I never knew.

Yet, I still wanted more pictures. The curiosity would aggravate me. I found more pictures lying around the trash near where I found my first magazine. I felt compelled to pick them up, so I wiped them off and stuck them inside my coat. This set of magazines was more graphic, showing more revealing pictures. Heart pumping, mind anxious, body sweating, I became a willing vessel for pornography to pour into me all that it had to offer through those pictures.

I felt rejected and confused. I would go to church, hear the message, and watch people go forward to receive Christ. I felt like I didn't belong there. I felt ashamed and afraid. And I knew God was not pleased with my behavior.

It wasn't the pictures itself that bothered me, but rather the thought of getting caught with them that worried me the most. I now had this habit of wanting more pictures. I wanted to stop, but I couldn't. So why not? I could have thrown them away, but I didn't. I thought I needed them.

Once I accepted this behavior as normal, I decided I would have to investigate these sexual desires more in depth, talking with my friends, reading more on the subject. I decided to read the letters that people sent in. Maybe I could learn from them. So I did, and I was starting to feel better. These people seemed to be very normal. The articles were well-written, using full sentences and more intelligent language than I was used to. I grew bolder in risk-taking in order to stay in touch with my sexual desires.

One day, I found a way to sneak a book into church and read it during the sermon. I hid the outer pictures inside my Bible or hymnal so the church ladies couldn't see what I was really reading. I enjoyed myself so much that the church service seemed shorter than usual. Although I was reading my articles, the pastor's words would still somehow seep into my heart. I would hear him say, "Come to the altar. Ask the Lord to forgive you before it's too late."

For a moment, that familiar guilt returned, but only until I walked out the church doors. I never knew why I had these feelings. I was just told that if I committed bigger sins, I would lose my salvation. Could this be one of those bigger sins?

I was growing up much faster than most boys in junior high. What I wanted from these magazines, I tried to get. No matter the cost, I would satisfy my mind and body, at first in small ways, but as I grew, my behavior worsened.

In those days the girls wore miniskirts above the knees. I was so curious, I let my eyes wander. My mind was still so young that I couldn't figure out my feelings. My hormones were on fire, but instead of asking questions, I tried to figure it out on my own. I searched the magazines for answers. They had the answers, but their answers justified my behavior. My church taught firmly: premarital sex bad, marriage good. But the magazine articles said that the only way to stop the crazy feeling was to do it. So, was it OK to have sex and not be married? Who was right? Who was wrong?

## A Mother's Answer

Still today, I cannot figure out how my mom knew that I was struggling with puberty. So, what did she do? She made an appointment with our family doctor to talk to me about these feelings. When I was a young boy, talking about sex was taboo. As the doctor advised me on some things, I simply looked away and ignored him. My mind was thinking about the articles in my magazines. I was thinking about all the advice that people had written in. No doctor was going to tell me any different. I was resigned to reading and looking at the pictures. I liked how it made me feel, and as a growing boy, I wasn't about to stop it. From the doctor to our pastor, I kept going for counseling.

"Now what, Mom? Wasn't the doctor enough? Now you must embarrass me in front of the preacher. What are you telling him about me?" Did my mom know about the pictures that I kept hidden?

At my appointment with the preacher, I sat ignoring him, looking away, like I had with our doctor. I felt uncomfortable with the questions I wanted to ask him. I wish I had been able to drum up enough courage to accept the help that God was placing in my life at an early age. I had it in my mind that I could quit when I got bored.

But I never did. This small voice continued to warn me of the consequences lying in wait on the path ahead. I kept my magazines hidden in our garage, which was so old that my mom would never go out there because she feared the mice. Not me! I loved to trap the little rodents. I was tall enough that I could stand on an old metal bucket and hide my magazines in the rafters. The old garage full of mice and dirty pictures was perfect for me. There, I felt a power much bigger than me trying to take over my mind, my emotions, my life.

I set myself up to be vulnerable. I didn't understand what that meant. I had two attributes that cause men to lust—thought and sight. In an instance, it seemed, I had been changed from innocent and vulnerable into a willing vessel for Satan to manipulate.

I had no idea what my future would hold, but God did.

But like many people then and now, I thought I could live my life any way I wanted and deal with sin when I got older. Worse, I still wasn't convinced 100% that what I was doing was wrong.

My conscience was fighting over what to do with my magazines. At times I wanted to throw them away, but the urge to keep them overpowered me to toss them away. I didn't understand how Christians could grow in the faith. All I thought about was the right now, the present. I didn't consider how my actions would hurt people who loved me.

My mom was a moral parent, although her persistent belief in a better me irritated me. Sometimes, she would never give up. Much to my surprise, she would always tell my dad after finding me "misbehaving." Those conversations would inevitably lead to my father whipping me with a belt when he came home from work. Being woken up at night and chased by a belt I could never outrun was no fun. Bitterness took root toward my dad. I can remember this feeling vividly even today. Why was I getting beat? I guess I deserved it, but I longed for my dad to talk to me instead of beating me to death.

From that time on, I hated my dad. I would get my answers somewhere else. Instead of beating me, I wanted my dad to love me, to explain to me why puberty was so hard for me. I needed to hear love, understanding, and support for change to take place. It never came. What I received was, "Don't do that. You'll go to hell. You're bad."

My mom would later tell me, "That's the way it was in those days."

So, a generation with sexual addition would grow up to be what we are today—perverted.

Two

# Choices

I was looking for role models I could follow, but I found few. I was living by my emotions, by what felt good. My life was about the feelings, not about any consequences. What kept going through my young mind was, *It feels good, so it must be good.* I never looked outside that circle. I never understood that what I was hearing in the music I chose to listen to or seeing in the pictures in my magazine were going to eventually affect my behavior. I kept hearing that my actions were wrong.

Kids today are more inundated with their peers telling them how to live. Some commit suicide because they can't live up to their parents' ideals contrasted with their peers telling them to "be loose" and "anything goes."

"When you die, then you will find out the truth." That's true! When we die, the truth will be revealed, but on whose side will you be? It will be one or the other. I knew that back then, but I was willing to gamble with my life. I believed God would understand that I couldn't help myself.

## Heaping Coals

One of my childhood homes had a coal furnace, and my brother and I would get stuck shoveling coal every morning. Sure, it kept us warm during the day, but by the time we woke up in the morning, the house was freezing because the fire had burned out the coals.

One morning, when it was cold inside, I thought of paying my dad back for the beatings. I walked downstairs, picked up numerous shovelfuls of coal, and put them in the furnace. When I saw the furnace turning bright red, I knew I was in trouble, so I ran off to my friend's house, figuring my dad would blame my younger brother.

I later returned home from my friend's house as if everything was normal. However, what I saw inside our home was anything but normal. Coal had smudged all over the inside of the house even though the windows and doors had been opened to allow fresh air to clean out the smoke.

When I saw my dad, he was as red as the furnace had been when I snuck out the back door hours earlier. The coal had ruined the paint on the walls, and while my brother and I blamed each other for the mischief, I realized I was the one who needed to get away from our home. I had wanted my dad to treat me like a son, not an annoyance like I felt I was. If my family couldn't show me that they loved me, I would go where I knew there was love.

## To Grandmother's House I Go

And so, I went to visit my grandparents, my dad's parents. Strong believers in Christ, my grandparents were great examples. Their values were unmeasurable. So much love and peace flowed from their home that often us kids would fight over who would stay with them on weekends.

Grandma would always have the radio on top of the refrigerator tuned in to a Christian station, and though they didn't own a television back then, my grandma would always find something for us to do, like pulling weeds in her garden. I remember one time she was working in the garden, thinking I was sleeping, but instead I was listening to soft rock 'n roll. When she figured out what I was listening to, much to my surprise, she walked over to turn off the radio. She didn't yell at me, beat me, or belittle me. She simply commented, "You shouldn't be listening to that stuff. It's bad for you. Come out and help me pull weeds. I will make some strawberry shortcake later."

Grandma made most everything from scratch, and when we had family gatherings at my grandparents' house, Grandpa would make ice cream by using his ice cream maker. It might have been the old, crank style, but we always looked forward to helping him with it. When my arm got tired, another kid would take over. Not to be left out of the fun of making dessert, Grandma would gather us and add delicious toppings to flavor the vanilla ice cream. It was another simple pleasure I remembered from my life back then.

Grandpa took great pride in helping with the upkeep of the church he attended. When he would go to his church to straighten up the landscape or clean inside, I would tag along, hoping I could help mow the grass or clean the pews. One way or another, God kept me within the shadow of his sight.

How could I have ever been so mischievous with great grandparents on both my mom and dad's sides? Good question.

My other grandma, on my mom's side, also had great faith. She also had great patience and a certain kind of indescribable, unwavering love for all her grandchildren. However, there was a great difference between my mom's and my dad's sides of the family. My dad's side was the more spiritual of the families, and my mom's side was the wilder bunch. They drank, smoked cigarettes, and often sat around the table squawking about a bunch of useless subjects that a kid would never understand.

In hindsight, I can see where my truck driving skills came from. My grandma lived in a small studio apartment with a recliner and a small TV on her stand where she kept her pills. She suffered from arthritis and other ailments, yet she rarely complained. We often picked her up on Sundays to take her out to dinner.

She always kept the cookie jar full of cookies for us kids. The one greatest passion she had was her faith in Christ. Most times when we came over, she would have her Bible lying on her lap; she would be either sleeping or reading it. Her favorite programs on TV were the *Tonight Show starring Johnny Carson* and the *Lawrence Welk Show*.

In the evenings, we always smelled the aroma from the bakery ovens baking fresh bread. Grandma would send someone down to the bakery's back door to knock on the door and buy the bread fresh from the oven. When one of us returned with the fresh bread, we all sat at her little kitchen table and ate it with watermelon. Those days were special to me also.

She demanded respect for God and was especially hard on my one uncle who smoked, drank, and used vulgar language. One time I recall her throwing him out of her apartment for using God's name in vain. She yelled, "Elmer, I want you to leave right now and don't come back until you clean up your mouth! I will not have you talk like this in front of the kids."

It was good for me to see a grown man brought into subjection by his frail, disabled mother who had this powerful dedication to Christ. Although I didn't recognize the spiritual value of what I was witnessing at the time, I can now see the Lord was giving me an example of how our behavior reflects our hearts.

I also didn't understand at the time how she could thank God during her pain. From a cane, to crutches, to a walker, and then finally her recliner, she never ceased to give God praise.

"One day, Bobby," I recall her saying, "you are going to preach."

I never told her what I thought about that, but inside, I was replying, "No way, Grandma. I'm going to have my fun first, then maybe I'll think about it."

By this time, I had already convinced myself that my sexual desires and behaviors were justified—not right, but not wrong, either. I would not disrespect or disappoint my grandma, but I knew the preacher's life was not a direction I was ready or willing to take.

Later, I would have the chance to attend a Christian college in Michigan, but by that time with Vietnam lurking in the shadows of many American homes, I had already abandoned any goals to live my best life. I figured I would be drafted into the war sooner or later. One day, Grandma told Mom she was tired of all the pain. She wanted to go home.

All Grandma's children were grown, my mom being the baby of the family. Grandma told her she wanted to go to heaven and that she would see her mom there. She asked the Lord if he would let her come home. Three days later, Grandma went home to be with the Lord. Now my mom and grandma are together forever.

# Choices

St. Joseph's River was one of the favorite spots where my friends and I loved to swim. The current was calm most days, and we hung a rope from a tree that we used to fly into the water. I learned how to swim at Boy Scout camp during the summers. I had always loved the water, swimming, canoeing, and fishing.

In Boy Scouts, we went camping in the winter, sitting by the fire to keep warm. Each of us would bring our favorite can of soup, which was poured into a clean metal trash can that stewed on the fire.

The Scouts were another chance to get rid of my magazines, but something kept me from throwing them all away. I felt like the pictures in the magazines were part of me, like a family. I couldn't get the images out of my mind.

When I was bored at home, my friends and I liked to pull a few pranks now and then. I called cabs and ordered pizzas for people that knew nothing about it. I would crack up laughing and thrilled of watching people's reactions when the cab honked the horn or when guys walked back to their cars with undelivered pizzas.

One night, a friend of mine and I planned a prank on someone on our way home from a Boy Scout meeting. I knocked on a lady's door. When she answered, I said, "Excuse me, ma'am. I'm on a scavenger hunt. Do you have an egg I can have?"

"Sure, young man, hold on," the unsuspecting women replied.

My friend Kevin walked up as she handed me the egg, but I purposely dropped it on her porch.

"You idiot! Why did you drop it? That was the last thing we needed!" Kevin feigned surprise.

"Hold on, guys. I'll get you another one."

"Thank you, ma'am." Kevin and I chuckled.

Walking away, we turned back and threw the egg at her house. After running home, I sat in my bedroom and continued laughing at how we got that lady good. By the time I fell asleep, I had started to feel bad about the night, regretting that she would have to clean up after us.

## Boy Interrupted

I remember the day President John F. Kennedy was assassinated. I was having lunch in school when over the loudspeaker I heard the news: "President Kennedy has been shot. School is excused for the day."

I returned home to watch news coverage on television. Hearing next that the man who shot our president was shot also, I felt fear and insecurity. What else might happen?

Loneliness clouded my home life because my parents were glued to the TV, watching the news reports of JFK's assassination and funeral. I heard the drum cadence playing in unison and the clip-clop of the horse-drawn carriage. Americans were weeping for their leader, and I felt unsafe for the first time in my life.

America was changing. Rock 'n roll music, drugs, smoking pot, and free love were the themes of the day. The Vietnam War was growing while daily protests were broadcast over television and radio. The news scared me. *What if I get drafted? I'll get shot. I'll die.* Though I was only in junior high, I knew I was moving closer to the very real possibility, even probability, of the draft. When reporters described

Russia having missiles pointed directly at us from Cuba, war stayed at the forefront of the mind.

I was also scared about what was waiting for me in high school. Freshmen were picked on, so I had to be tough. I did grow up fast by reading from the minds of adults in my magazines.

Soon it was time for me to abandon my junior high school days, along with the pranks and cute little girls, Boy Scouts, and my best friend. During this turmoil, my America changing, I began to see some hope for my struggle with sexual desires and inappropriate behaviors. *Maybe I can start a new life, find new friends, and not keep these magazines hidden all the time.*

I thought I could throw the magazines away, but high school was a step on the path toward Vietnam. Then that voice inside, the one that I should have silenced long before high school, spoke to me again, "What's the use in giving up the magazines? You're going to die anyway."

I became a bitter young man with adult magazines that gave me temporary relief, a relief that was never good enough. My mind was filling with what I was reading—perversion, pornography. What seemed great, enjoyable, and normal, was destroying me.

As I began to mature physically, so did my mind. My conscience sometimes held up a red flag, but I figured out how to run stop sign after stop sign. That change would begin in high school, where I experienced more freedom, dances, fun, girls, sports, and parties. When it came to my studies, however, I would be lazy. Thus, it would take five years and three months for me to finish my high school education. My next adventure in high school set the stage for many huge bad decisions that I would regret. Yes—memories and scars.

But for now I was still living the huge gap between junior high and high school. A part of me couldn't wait to begin high school, but the other side wanted to stay young. Though I had hard times at home, I went to church more often.

I love to look back at what I learned in Vacation Bible School. The first time for me was in a vacant house, where we always had Kool-Aid and cookies. I remember the flannel pictures our teacher would use to illustrate the lessons. I had no excuse for being lazy. I was being raised to understand how a Christian should behave, but I didn't understand it back then. Now as an adult, I can see how much those lessons did affect me.

My mind would wonder, "So, why all the drama over these magazines?" "Why are these women posing nude?" "Why are there so many magazines coming out?" "What is their purpose?"

It was important for me to be accepted by someone, especially the girls. Being in junior high was rough for some of us: the president's assassination, the Vietnam war, smoking marijuana becoming more popular, and drinking flavored vodka to get drunk. These things were just beginning in my preteen years.

My generation back then would never comprehend the technology today. We were taught about the advancements that might happen. But drones? No way. Man going to the moon? Are you serious? In between *The Flintstones* and *The Jetsons*, our generation would invent automatic appliances and more advanced cars with power steering. While in the preteen age, we put a square small box in our pocket with wires that went between our radio, and this uncomfortable device that kept falling out of our ears was called an AM radio with ear plugs.

Upon entering high school, I was about to leave behind the simple way of life. My peers and I wanted to explore whatever we could get our hands on. Music made sense. We could understand the simple English language. I am amazed how many ads on TV still use the music of the early sixties.

Yes, we are called baby boomers. Times do change, and each generation has its ups and downs. I embrace my generation, because I believe that's when the big changes began. It began to change with the music, TV, drugs, and sexual experimentation. I was in a rush to experiment as much as I could. It seemed like fun. Now I would be going through the biggest change in my life. I believe that my high school years made the biggest difference in my life.

I listened to music that would tell me how to smoke dope, and Jefferson Airplane would sing a song to ask "Alice" when she was high because she was strung out on drugs. Another song was about "Mother's little helper," a woman taking her pills just to make it through the day.

It was this generation in the sixties that would change the course of sanity once and for all. We would get closer to that line of no return. Drugs would be legalized; sex would be for whatever you wanted it to be. Divorce would be as easy as drinking water. Our generation performed the first legal abortion in America. We were running away from the God who was blessing and protecting us. We had this misconception that God was busy so we could sneak in a little bit of fun. God wouldn't notice.

That is what was waiting for me in high school. I had no choice but to go through it, so all I wanted to do was dance through it, just skimming enough information to slide by. And that's what I did.

It was time to graduate from Nuner Junior High School. Graduation was always just after Memorial Day, with all its parades and celebrations. I said goodbye to my friends because my family was moving closer to Riley High School. It was there that I would be tempted to make changes in my life that would affect myself and others.

Three

# Ninth and Tenth Grades

During my freshman year, I met new friends who viewed more explicit photos. Although the shadow of uncertainty regarding the Vietnam War, racial riots, and protests hovered over me, I managed to continue my spiral into the darkness of pornography.

By this time, most of my friends had lost their virginity, but not me, so I began to feel left out. My magazines were telling me that it was normal to have sex, so I knew I had to quickly become normal.

High school was way different than junior high. My teachers always loved to get us students involved in class. I was embarrassed when they pointed and ask me questions since I hardly ever did my homework. I had a hard time concentrating on my books. I always tried to avoid my teachers by pretending that I was reading my book, putting my head in my hands, trying not to have eye contact with them. Every time I would look at them, they seemed to ask me a question. Then I felt stupid because I didn't know the answer.

It took me three years to pass one year of English and history. Today, I love history. I love to dream about what it must have been like to live in an earlier era. My mom would always tell me: "Bob Jr., you can do it! You're very smart. You're just lazy. By the way, where's your homework?"

"I forgot it in my locker," I would repeatedly reply.

"Of course you did, on purpose no doubt. I better see it when you come through the door, or I'm going to call your school counselor." Though I didn't notice her relentlessly dogging me about my inner issues, she definitely pursued my educational issues at the highest level. Countless times my mother would call my counselor and teachers to check on my grades, behavior, and so on. Annoying as her pursuit was to me, my mother's compassion coupled with the patience and kindness of my counselor was the main reason I earned my high school diploma. They never gave up on me. Although I should have graduated in 1968, I ended up graduating in 1969, the same year as my brother, after I completed summer school to get my full credits. It would take me five years and three months to complete high school.

Talk about embarrassing! Taking so long to graduate sure didn't help my self-esteem much. By the end of high school, I was directing the bitterness from my earlier years toward my siblings and my parents (although most of it was directed toward my dad).

## Fast Times

Though I didn't know at that time that I would need five years to complete high school, I did notice the time moving quickly. I regret ignoring the advice of so many adults during those years: "Enjoy today, because you might not be here tomorrow." I wish I had taken the time to enjoy the simple pleasures, such as gardening with my grandmother.

Climbing trees with friends was soon replaced with loud, distasteful music and a promiscuous society. Sex replaced love for many and was as common and easily accessible as alcohol and cigarettes. Soon I learned how to think and talk dirty with the guys about girls in our classes. The new adult books and magazines helped my friends and me learn how to speak and act on unthinkable thoughts. What I had been exposed to in my early years now had a free and open platform on which to flourish.

However, I wasn't as experienced as my friends who'd had sex by the time they were fourteen. This made me feel embarrassed and angry. Here I was going on fifteen and nothing had happened. I had a better chance dreaming about the girls in my magazines than getting a girlfriend of my own.

I started turning to my friends for some tips. One of my friends shared how he was able to meet a girl on the phone. We had party lines in those days, so we could sometimes hear other people's phone calls. "But how did you get her number?" I asked.

"By mistake. I was dialing a wrong number, and it rang busy. I was listening to some girls on the other line. I could still hear the busy signal, but I started yelling through the phone, asking the girls for their number. I got one. Look, her name is Steph. I wrote it down."

"What's the number? Let me try," I nudged. "Maybe I can get lucky."

"Let's go to my house. My mom's working. We can try it there."

Once at his house, I somehow got distracted by his guitar. "Wow, you have a guitar. That is so cool. Let me hear you play it," I inquired, clearly distracted and not remembering our focus of calling girls.

"OK, I will after we talk to some girls." Mike picked up

the phone and dialed. "Hello, Hello. Can you hear me? This is Mike. What's your name?"

"Gloria," the girl on the other end of the line said.

"How old are you?" asked Mike.

"I'm fifteen; you?"

"Me and my friend are both fifteen. Do you have a friend there with you?"

"Yeah, but she's fourteen. Is that OK?"

"Yeah, why not. You want to meet downtown later? In about two hours?"

"I think so. Give me your number. I'll call you back in fifteen minutes," Gloria replied as she hung up the phone.

Mike and I became buddies. We were like guys standing on the corner looking for chicks or calling them. Our main transportation was walking. No matter the distance, we were out to meet girls. I was always shy, but he wasn't, so I learned from him how to manipulate and trick girls into playing around. I learned how to use their emotions to win them over.

Right on time, fifteen minutes later, Gloria called back. We arranged to meet the girls downtown, where we hung around, held hands, and tried to fight off our raging hormones. At the touch of a girl's hand, my thoughts raced. I had never felt anything so soft. Was this real love or puppy love? I used to think I was in love every time a girl looked at me.

Because this girl went to a different school, she never knew about me flunking my way through school, which emboldened me to act more liberally around her, not always worrying about what a loser she might think I was for not doing well in school.

Ninth and Tenth Grades

## Freshman Blues

I had a hard time adjusting in my freshman year, which was a disaster, both at home and at school. The boys would tease me in front of the girls. I wasn't the best dressed kid in school. In fact, many times I would try to hide the holes in my socks from everyone. Inevitably, some boy would see them and chide me for the rest of the school day. The more they teased me, the angrier I became.

Yes, I was that loner in ninth grade, the one who walked to school alone, walked the halls alone, and walked home from school alone. And there, at home, I kept to myself. I yearned for attention, but I began spending so much time alone, I wasn't sure if I would know how to socialize.

Looking to find my place in society throughout this awkward year, I tried out for freshman sports but was rejected. "Not good enough, kid," I recall hearing more than once. I didn't "fit in" with most people, guys or girls, and at home, I fought with my brother and sisters.

My younger brother was shy, a trait that seemed to appeal to the girls, as they tended to shower him with attention. He also had many friends, and, as the classic tale of good brother/bad brother goes, he was an excellent student, completely opposite of me.

I still attended church, although it did not make much difference in the emptiness I was feeling. I felt like no one loved me. People my age rarely sat with me or greeted me in church. I joined the church youth baseball team, hoping to make friends, but I kept dropping fly balls and feeling stupid for doing so. Turns out, even church teams like to win, so I was placed in the lineup only when they had run up the score so high that losing wasn't an option, even with me in the game.

## It Only Takes One Look

I was searching for answers in church. I wanted to know why I felt so bad reading my magazines. *Who am I hurting? I would ask myself. I'm not forcing anyone else to join me.* After all, I read the magazines alone. *All I am doing is looking at pictures. Besides, maybe they'll help me hook up with girls so I won't always be alone.* Yet every second I spent looking at the magazines, I felt overwhelmed with guilt and frustration. I didn't understand why I was so driven to return to them nearly every time I was alone.

I wanted Dad and son time. I wanted my father to help me with these feelings and my thoughts, especially when I knew I couldn't just come out and ask a stranger from church or my counselor. What would a woman in church think about me?

I was trying to find my place among my peers and failing miserably. Everything around me seemed to work against me, so I began to trust no one. These feelings seemed to funnel me right into the swirling madness of my magazines. When I was in a sour mood, I retreated to where I was alone with my magazine girls. Sometimes, though, I would crawl out my bedroom window and sit on the roof, looking up and wondering if God could see me messing up my life. Often, I was told not to sit on the roof, but I wouldn't listen.

Eventually I was moved downstairs in the corner of the basement, in my own private space. The only bad part was the footsteps walking back and forth upstairs. No headsets existed in those days to block out the noise. One day, I heard an argument between my parents about how poorly I was doing in school.

"I got a call from Riley High School about Bob Jr. failing his classes," Mom told Dad. "They are concerned about no

## Ninth and Tenth Grades

homework being turned in. They want to keep him after school to help him. What should we do?"

"Ground him for a week" was my dad's answer. That was easy.

"That's not the solution." My mom prompted for more effort from my dad.

"Then you handle it." Case closed. That was always his answer: "Then you handle it." Stick it on Mom.

Dad missed many opportunities to engage in my life, to sit down and encourage me. How I would have loved to hear him say, "Bob, don't quit school like I did in the seventh grade. You can be anything you want if you put your mind to it. You can always talk to me. I'm here for you."

Many parents think they can argue or hide their behavior from their children. But kids are smart. They figure out that Mommy and Daddy don't like each other very much when they fight often. Some children may hold it inside, then release it when they become adults. Some may act out by running away from home, doing drugs, having sex, or committing crimes.

Children need to feel safe at home, not threatened by violence or emotionally abandoned by their parents. I didn't know how I would turn out, but I knew at the time I needed to get away as much as possible from school and my parents.

Gone, it seemed, in an instant, my freshman year led me to conclude that I needed money. During the summer break, I got a job working at a grocery store restocking shelves, where I also acquired the skill to steal liquor through a crack in the furnace pipe. The furnace wasn't working, so I would come back after work to retrieve the vodka I had stashed in the pipe before I left work.

I didn't drink the alcohol I stole. Instead, I used it to attract friends. Yes, I stole booze just to make new friends. My social plan ended abruptly when a neighbor saw us and reported me to my boss. Of course, I was fired, but then my boss had to tell my parents what I had done. For this special lesson, I was grounded for a month, although I didn't let their petty punishment stop me from sneaking out of the house when I wanted to.

## Sophomore Blues

I became very rebellious my sophomore year. The goofy freshman was no more. After all, I had now made a few new friends who liked to drink, talk to girls, and, like me, look at porn. We became very close, spending most of our time together, doing exactly what we felt like doing.

None of us owned a car, but you wouldn't be able to tell by our hanging out where everyone cruised the town. I would stay out after curfew, knowing that when I got home, my mother would be sitting on the sofa with a worried and angry look on her face, asking, "Where have you been? What time do you think curfew is, young man?"

"I know, I know," I would say, waving her off.

"Don't you talk to me that way! Go to your room."

Poor Mom. She tried, but I had no intention of following any curfew. Mom began to suspect what other rebellious behaviors I might be doing. She snooped in my dresser looking for drugs, questioned me about every detail of my life, and warned me daily about bad girls.

One thing she did not ask or suspect during this time was about my pornography habit. Other things Mom could find out, but I was protective of my magazines. The magazines and books were telling me how to, when to, and that there was more to just looking at girls.

I was truly addicted, and seemingly nothing would help me. I loved reading and looking at porn more than I did my schoolbooks. I was in trouble and didn't realize it at the time. My attitude began to change during my sophomore year.

All I wanted was to be accepted by someone, most importantly by those who were popular, but I soon was coaxed into being accepted by those who played pranks and skipped school. I wanted to have fun. I had friends who loved to hang out with girls.

The friends I hung out with also had family problems. One of my friends had a deceased dad. Another of my friends had a dad who drank heavily. He hardly ever stayed at home because his dad would beat him when he got drunk.

My dad might have been stubborn and worked long hours, but he was faithful in trying to supply for our needs. I also was stubborn. By that time, I didn't care how much he worked. During my high school years, the less I saw of my dad, the better. But part of me still wished I could spend time with him alone, not with my uncles, who usually happened to be there when I finally got time with him.

In my sophomore year I tried to impress the girls in school. I kept trying to talk to them on the busy signal phone. I had no real goals. My problem was, I wouldn't listen to anyone. I thought I knew better, and I was always blaming my parents. I was jealous watching other boys holding girls' hands.

That year in school crawled slowly by. I didn't have the will to study or do my homework. I just wanted to mess around at my friend's house, riding his moped and listening to rock 'n roll. Every hour we heard on the news about Vietnam. I couldn't figure out why our troops were there dying.

"Where is this Vietnam?" I asked one day, sitting in my friend's living room.

"I have no idea, man, but I bet we get drafted. What, are you afraid of getting killed over there?"

"Kind of."

"Yeah, so I figure, why go to school if I'm going to get drafted? What's the use?"

From that time on, I didn't care much about school, church, or life because I figured I would someday be forced to go to Vietnam and would die there. I was determined to live for today. And I wasn't alone in my thinking. Songs on the radio repeated the same types of lyrics about living for today, being free to be and do whatever you wanted to do.

My friends also shared the belief that our lives would soon be ended because of the war. I hung out with those who had little doubt about the future. When I was with my friends, I talked and acted like them. I developed a vulgar mouth, and while I attended church very little, I did continue to attend Sunday school. Even in my rebellion, I never fit in. When I was alone, I would often think about the words of that youth pastor, "You could die at any time. I could die at any time. Now would be a good time to give your life to the Lord before getting drafted and shot to death."

These thoughts I shook off quickly, but they would appear again and again. I was taught in church that some sins were worse than other sins. The bigger sins would be held against me unless I confessed them right away. In other words, you could lose your salvation if you forgot to confess the bigger sins.

## Ninth and Tenth Grades

*So which sins are worse?* I wondered. *How do I keep track of them? What if I forget and go to bed without confessing them? What if I die in my sleep? Then I will go to hell. Where's that at? Is it a bad place? Does that mean I will go to hell because I read these magazines?*

By now, the magazines had a hold on me that I could not shake. I was too much into them. I wouldn't give them up. I observed the girls in school, then I would get more magazines that showed me more of what I wanted to see, with less clothing and greater variety.

I continued to neglect my schoolwork and hung out with guys who took pride in the fact that they had no hope for their futures. My friends did whatever they wanted and went wherever they wanted. I soon became like those guys.

Four

# Junior Year at Riley

At the beginning of my junior year in high school, nothing changed the first month, but something in my thinking was different. I started feeling guilty for having the magazines. I didn't understand it, but I was on the verge of waging a spiritual battle. I would soon be living two lives, switching from one side to the other.

Finally, something good happened. I had a chance to go to driver's education. It was so much fun. Driving became natural to me, but I never knew that I would have a future in it. After completing drivers ed class, I went down to the DMV and took my driving test.

I was on top of the hill. Life was good. Now for my first car—a Studebaker that had to be towed by my dad and my uncle. I don't know how my uncle got it, but it had to be repaired. My car lasted for about five months, and then it had to be towed to the junkyard.

I remember letting my friends write messages or their names on my car. Sometimes I drove it to my favorite spot at the park and read my magazines. The car shook when I drove it, but it still ran (barely) for five months.

After that, I was back walking and taking the bus. My high school counselor did her best to keep me on track with my schoolwork. I listened but ignored what she was saying to me. *One more year and I'll be finished with school.* So I thought! Some of my friends were getting cars, but my dad told me that if I wanted a car, I would have to get a job and buy the car and insure it myself.

So, that's what I did. I got a job at a root beer stand down the street. It was a fun job, until one day my mom showed up to work at the same place. With her looking over my shoulder, I couldn't be myself chasing the girls, so I quit that job and found my next one at a full-service gas station.

Then my dad did something that shocked me. Now that I had a responsible job, he went out on a limb and financed my next car, a 1963 Chevrolet Bel Air. I considered this my first real car.

After awhile on the job pumping gas, checking fluids, and cleaning windshields, my boss taught me how to read the stick that showed how much gas was in the tanks the customers pumped from. Rather than taking his trust in me seriously, I figured out how I could cheat the figures and keep my car full of gas for free. I also figured out how to fix the readings on the pump that would roll over to the next shift. I learned how to rig the system and cheat my boss. I obviously had integrity issues that extended beyond my magazines. My cheating lasted a short while until I was caught by the owner. He could have made life incredibly difficult for me right then, but rather than call the police, the owner fired me and let me figure out my wrong for myself. Unfortunately, I never told my dad I was fired, but instead, I told him that I had quit.

I reacted by simply retreating downstairs to my room and pulling out my magazines. I always knew if someone would be coming downstairs by their footsteps and could hide the magazines in time. Every time I needed something to calm me down and take me away from being responsible, I went to my own little world of fantasies.

In my world, I made up role-plays that included these girls. I made them my girlfriends. After being fired, I considered myself more of a failure, even though I knew it was the consequence of me stealing from my boss. I lost my car and my insurance and blamed my dad for not continuing to pay for my insurance. I told him I would pay him back, but he didn't believe me. *Yeah, right! Of course he's not going to do that for me! I'm the black sheep of the family. I can't do anything right in his eyes. I fail in school. I have no girlfriends, I lost my car. I'm a thief, and I'm going to die in Vietnam. So, who cares? I don't.*

Bitterness and frustration began to manifest more through my behavior in school. I started fighting, usually over a girl. I wasn't going to take it anymore—not by guys in school, my dad, my brother, or anyone else. I stood up for myself, even when I was wrong.

I made excuses for being lazy in school. I learned from one of my friends how to skip classes by using street fire alarms. If my buddy wanted me to skip with him, he would wait till I was passing from one class to another, then pull the alarm. When the school emptied, I would leave. We did the same thing when we needed to get back into school.

Another way of skipping school was to write out each other's excuse and sign our parent's name. When we got caught, we received a three-day suspension.

The more my mom cared, the more I reacted the opposite and got angry. Deep in my rebellion and emotional mess, I didn't want my mom to care. I wasn't worth caring about. No one could talk sense into me, not even my beloved grandparents. When my report card came out, I refused to show it to my mom. So, she went to the school to get it.

The two places I didn't want to be were home and the classroom, but I loved sporting events because I could watch the cheerleaders. I recall a set of twins I had my eyes on, which only led to disappointment when I found out that their boyfriends were football players.

## Girls, Boys, Friends, and the War

Toward the end of my junior year I became interested in another girl that I tried to befriend, but I soon learned that she too had a boyfriend. Determined to give this one a try regardless of her boyfriend, I worked to show her that I was a better person than he was, since I knew him to not be a very nice person.

My perseverance paid off. We began spending a lot of time together even though she lived about three miles from our house. I either took the bus or walked to see her. Because I no longer had a car of my own, we had to double date. This inconvenience motivated me to take a job making bed frames at a wood shop.

I had to work long hours, but it was worth it to me even though I couldn't spend as much time with my girlfriend. Meanwhile, some of my classmates quit school and joined the military early by convincing their parents to sign an age waiver. Just thinking about dying scared me, so I quickly abandoned any thought of doing the same.

Sadly, the next year I heard about one of the guys being killed. I still didn't understand about the war, and hearing about his death fueled my hatred of the whole mess. The thought of enlisting after graduation entered my mind, if for no other reason than to join before they forced me via the draft.

My best friend Mike also got a job at the wood shop. After work, he and I hung out with friends who played in a band. Mike was the lead guitarist, and he had friends who played drums, rhythm guitar, and bass guitar. They were good enough to form a band. I became somewhat of a manager, trying to find gigs for them. The band did sock hops at school and a Polish wedding reception. I intended to learn how to play the drums because the drummer was a senior, soon to be drafted.

I tried to put my life together, but I still had this secret lusting for the girls in my magazines and the ones I saw at school. Even with a real girlfriend of my own, I wanted more. She wasn't enough because my mind had been altered with fantasies of what I read in those magazines. The preacher's words had come too late. That back-alley experience from my childhood had altered my life, and nothing could be done to turn it around now, or at least that's what I felt at the time.

One night my mom asked me about my girlfriend. She had learned that my cousin's husband had a niece, who was my girlfriend. This made her my second cousin, but not by blood. While confusing at the time and a little disturbing, the news didn't stop us from continuing our relationship. Mom would always snoop in and ask me personal questions. I tried to keep my mom away from my girlfriend. She might have meant well, but her questions embarrassed me in front of my girlfriend. Eventually, our family situation did affect our relationship, so we broke up and my girlfriend suggested that I go to a Bible college. Sounded like a great idea. That way I could stay out of the military, but I never ended up going.

In between my junior and senior years, I had to enroll in summer school to catch up on credits I needed to graduate. My mom thought I was going to school, but even then, I skipped school. I didn't care enough to even try. I continued to meet girls on the phone like Mike had taught me that one night at his house, and I went cruising Friday and Saturday nights, looking for girls.

Failure was part of my life. It seemed I failed at everything. I couldn't wait until I was twenty-one. Then no one would tell me how to live. Some of my friends opted to join the military instead of graduating, but my mother would never sign for me to go to war. She was going to make sure I graduated.

I knew that I was way behind in credits, so I thought I could make them up in wood shop and metal class. However, the two classes I needed to get my diploma were English and history. Mike and I decided to take home economics for the sole purpose of meeting more girls. Turned out, we were the only two guys in the class, and we liked those odds. After we passed the class, our teacher asked us why we had taken it in the first place.

Mike admitted, "We figured we would be the only guys in the class . . . to meet all the girls."

"Well, did you guys manage to get dates?"

"No, but it was fun."

In the junior year of high school, most students would begin making plans to go to college, but not me or my friends. Sure, going to college would get you four more years of freedom from the military, but I wasn't looking that far ahead, and why would I want to suffer through four more years when I hated to study now?

Then there were the draft dodgers who chickened out by going to Canada. I resented those guys who ran away instead of serving their country. That wasn't me.

Soon, it was time to order our senior class rings and get pictures taken for our yearbook. The class ring would cost $10 and the yearbook $5.00. Gas was $.29 a gallon. Prices have changed since then, but remember our pay was lower too.

I did a quick spot at McDonalds, where I worked for two months. My pay was $1.25 an hour. I still have the paystub. That was before inside dining. People would walk up to the window and order, then they had to eat in their cars. I wonder if that's how cruising began?

Five

# Senior Year

### Flunking Through

My senior year was mixed with racial riots, protesting of the war, and an overall uncertainty about our lives. *Why should I start caring about my classes now? Next month I must sign up for the draft. I will just have fun. I don't care anymore.* I still skipped classes and stayed away from my family as much as possible. When I was home, my friends came over, and we played football in the street. Life was boring, unless we made it interesting, such as pulling a prank such as the following one:

Mike: "Hey Bob, you want to play a prank on the fire station?"

Bob: "How?"

Mike: "Let's pull this fire alarm and hide in the bushes in the alley and see what happens."

Bob: "OK, but you pull it."

Mike pulled the alarm; we went running to the bushes. Off in the distance we could hear the sirens getting closer. They stopped at the alarm, saw no fire, reset the alarm, and left. On the way to my house, we decided to do it again. This time I pulled it and ran toward my house.

When we got close to the house, we heard more than one siren. This time, assisting the fire trucks were police cars.

They were looking for whoever had pulled the alarm. We hid downstairs in my room, hoping that no police would knock on the door. Luckily, none did.

Later, on the news, we heard the police were looking for whoever had pulled the alarms. "If we catch those responsible, they will wash our fire truck and police cars," the officer warned.

We laughed about it then, but the authorities didn't think it was so funny. This prank would be kept a secret between Mike and me for years.

In senior year, expectations should have been to graduate, but for me, I would face the consequences for my years of laziness in school.

In 1968, I could not graduate with the rest of my friends because I couldn't make up enough credits to graduate with my class. This might have been a big deal to most people, but for me, as was my normal attitude toward school back then, I didn't take academics seriously. On one hand, I knew I needed to graduate, but on the other hand, I didn't see a future in it.

Mom did not share my indifference about school. In fact, she was the only person who took my life seriously. Despite my attitude toward school, I did not quit. I tried to pass history and English. My mom wanted me to stay home more often, but when I wasn't in school, I wanted to be anywhere but home.

I liked to spend time at a school out in the country that had lights that lit an outdoor basketball court. Nobody ever bothered us when we played there. We were just a bunch of guys having fun before the war would split us up.

I remember meeting a girl who did not attend our school,

but her boyfriend did. When I saw them together, I couldn't believe my eyes. She was with the same guy I had taken my last girlfriend from. Something about her caught my interest, although I couldn't put my finger on it. I figured I would get her attention the same way I had gotten my ex-girlfriend's attention.

Soon after, I was in the hall at my locker when the boyfriend walked up to me and shoved me against my locker. He threatened, "If you look at my girlfriend one more time, I'm going to kick your butt."

"I don't think you can. I took your last girlfriend. Maybe I'll do it again."

"I'm going to kick your [bleep] after school. You better be in the back of the school. We'll settle this. If you're not there, I'll find you."

"Oh yeah, right. I'll be there taking your girl from you."

After school, we fought over Sue—no weapons, just good ol' fist fighting. I remember having him pinned against the fence, punching back and forth, when our wood shop teacher came running out the back door. We both ran off.

For the rest of the year we stayed away from each other, but I did manage to get his girl. There was something special about her. I knew she went to church a lot with her mom and grandmother, and like my grandparents, her grandma was a strict Christian. At the end of my senior year, I took Sue to my senior prom and then to Lake Michigan, where we built a fire and fell asleep on the beach. I had a lot of explaining to do when I took her home. I was falling in love with her because I knew she cared about me. She was a junior, and I was a senior. Then the bad news came.

## Senior Year, Again

My mom said, "I spoke with your counselor, and she suggested that we keep you back a year. You do not have enough credits to graduate. That's what too much fun does when you should be in school. You will only have to go half days."

"There's no way I'm going to graduate with my friends? They will be gone!"

"You're the only one to blame. You kept playing around, thinking you would graduate. Is it funny now? I didn't think so. You must pass English and history to graduate. They are mandatory."

"What if I don't?"

"Well, you're eighteen now. If you don't go back to school, you'll have to move out. If you're not serious about your education, then you're not serious enough about your life."

I knew she was right. But regardless of how right she was, I went downstairs to my magazines that I had hidden and escaped from this horrible news by looking at the pictures and reading the editorials. What I was reading was intense, spurring a greater curiosity in me to explore my sexual desires more in depth. It all seemed innocent now at the age of eighteen, but still my thoughts were driving me mad. Though I was dating a sweet girl whom I loved, the editorials were saying I could keep her and yet have more than her.

Not sure how exactly that would work out, I tucked this fantasy in my mind for later use. In school, the rumor went around that I had flunked. I had to take the embarrassment, especially the thoughts of graduating with my brother. I was older. I shouldn't have had to graduate with him.

After my senior year, I had to go to summer school again.

## Senior Year

Now almost nineteen, I felt worthless. I finally completed the necessary credits needed to get my diploma, but I was so embarrassed, I refused to walk down the aisle wearing my cap and gown. I was angry with myself, so Mom picked up my diploma at the school for me, and high school was finally over.

When I look back over those five years it took to graduate, I must give all the credit to my mother. Mothers have this unique empowered love for their children. Though I was stubborn, Mom saw right through me. She never gave up on me, and when I gave up on myself, she made me feel bad when she explained my failures to me. She wouldn't let me blame the family for messing up in school. Though the blame was mine, she still encouraged me and always told me that she loved me. When you are a kid, you don't want to hear how to change your behavior and live like you have a future.

Today, it is disturbing to hear about teenagers who run away, tearing apart their families and breaking their mother's heart. I just heard on the news today that two teenagers committed suicide in one week, in Aurora, Colorado. One was a senior, the other a junior, from two different schools. When you think your mom doesn't care, stop for a second and look back at all she has done for you. Even when you are indifferent with your mom, she will still be there for you with encouragement and support.

Yes, I know there are exceptions—mothers who abandon children to starvation, neglect, and abuse, but most mothers endure much heartache and sacrifice for their children. When you disrespect your mother, one day memories will come back, and pain will resurface. All those fun times I thought I had with my friends ended up being painful memories.

Where were they after I graduated? They pursued their own lives, and I was all alone. The fun was gone. The only one left was me. Often, kids think and live as if their high school fun will continue into adulthood, but life changes quickly, and only the prepared can weather the change maturely and successfully.

Playing through school is dangerous. Maybe you think no one cares, but God does. He did for me. Though I still didn't understand why God put up with me through school, the truth was he did. Don't play around with your education, because the only one to blame will be yourself.

I couldn't blame my failures on my parents. I couldn't blame them on my friends who convinced me to skip school and chase girls. Those pranks we did weren't funny and pointed to my own moral shortcomings. Maybe at the time they were funny, but what if there had been another fire somewhere? The firefighters might have been late getting there; people could have lost their lives.

Our culture still tries to convince us that what you do privately will not affect others. But that's a lie. Nothing is a secret. Somewhere, sometime, down the road the consequences will come. My time in school was fun and difficult. I finished school exactly the way I behaved: lazy and disrespectful to my parents, and disrespectful to my school for caring about me.

Now high school was behind me. The war was waiting. I still had Sue, and I still worked at the wood shop factory. I also still lived at home, but that was about to change.

## The Love I Rejected

I didn't like living at home, but what was I to do? I had nowhere to go. When I signed up for the draft, my number indicated that Uncle Sam didn't need me, so I continued to work. The boss's son and I became friends. We both wanted to join the service, but we were both too afraid of what could happen to us if we were sent to fight.

One day Sue mentioned to me that her grandma had an empty room upstairs where I could live. I happily accepted it, but leaving my house was difficult, because I knew my mom didn't want me to leave. She must have known in her heart that I would join the military.

What I wanted was to get away from my dad. As I was moving out, he tried to grab the TV from me, and then he grabbed my neck instead. I landed my elbow in his stomach. Then I looked him square in the eyes and said, "Don't you ever touch me again! I'm not your whipping boy. You ever grab me around my neck again, you will regret it."

I left home after arguing with my dad. I went to live in that little room at Sue's grandma's house. Every time her grandma went to church, she would invite me to join her. Sometimes I went with her and other times with Sue. I enjoyed going because the people were nice to me.

Sue's dad was different, though. He was into séances and belonged to a spiritualist church that sought out the dead. I didn't know it at the time, but the Lord was using Sue and her grandma to bring me back into church. I played the game, and that was what life was to me. A big game. There was one thing that I couldn't lose, however, and that was the decision I had made when I walked down the aisle, giving my life to Christ. Yet I still struggled with why I continued to love my adult magazines. In my mind, what I saw people doing in the magazines seemed fun and exciting.

I would pour out my heart to God: *Why do I have these*

## It Only Takes One Look

*guilty feelings after I look at them? Why do I get so attracted to them? Why do you make me feel so guilty after I look at them? Answer me, God. Why don't I want to get rid of them? What makes me keep them?*

I kept the magazines hidden in my room. My buddy at work would trade me for the latest issues, but one day he gave me a different type of magazine. It was an issue of a swinger's magazine. Bob thought it was funny, but I was curious. I had to know what that was. I didn't want to listen to the voice of God that I would hear in church. I had to put up a front so that nobody would discover my secrets, my filthiness, my magazines. I had to play church and then set aside the church and God when I left. Then I would indulge in my magazines and sinful thoughts.

One night, I noticed an advertisement for a number to call for a fun time. I didn't care about whether the woman on the other end of the phone was married. I figured she didn't care, so why should I. So, I called. As we talked, she explained to me that cheating on her husband was her choice because she liked being with other guys.

I played along, disregarding the fact that the Lord had blessed me with a nice girlfriend and a quiet place to live. I had everything going for me, so why would I ever go out and cheat on Sue? If I kept this a secret, no one would know. In my pursuit of the unknown, a new experience, I never considered that I would be cheating on my girlfriend. Under the influence of the Word of God being preached at church, my insides writhed in torment. Something was making me feel very guilty, but I felt it was too late to stop. I was too far gone to let go now. I was torn up inside.

After establishing a relationship with the married woman,

## Senior Year

I felt guilt when I went back to church. I had to adjust to life again. Instead of surrendering to the feelings inside that certainly beckoned me to live right, I simply learned how to tolerate and ignore them. I loved going to church, but I loved my immoral life too. I fell in love with Sue and eventually quit seeing the married woman because I knew it would hurt Sue if she ever found out about us. When you play on Satan's terms, you are in for a gruesome, evil experience. Pleasures are meant to entice, but convictions afterward are awful. I used to tell Sue and God that I loved them. I acted like it all the time, especially in church. I put up a front, making people think I was this kind, loving young man, but deep down I knew I was sinning.

One night in church, the preacher was speaking about eternal salvation through what Jesus Christ did on the cross. He said that all my sins—past, present, and future—were forgiven. As I ingested the words that preacher spoke, as if directly at me, I stood up and walked down the aisle again, believing that I had lost my salvation. Then, a thought hit me, *You mean I can have my magazines and still be saved and go to heaven? Wow! This is great.*

Nobody told me upfront what the consequences would be when you do not listen to the Lord, that my heart would be ripped apart from convictions, that it would cost so much for me to finally listen to what God said and to obey him. All I could think about at the time was this so-called freedom to sin but still go to heaven. If you think for a minute that as a child of God you can get by with deliberate sinning without consequences, you are wrong. You can only test and tempt God for so long. He is a jealous God and will not be mocked. God is holy and will not have fellowship with sin. My spiritual journey began at the altar. It began at the cross.

Before I continue my journey, it is important to explain to you that no matter what Satan tempted me with, he could never change my mind on who Jesus was. I believed on the cross and on Jesus's death, burial, and resurrection. I had given my life to Christ. As you read this book, remember, I was and always will be a child of God. Nothing can separate me from him, and Romans 8:35 declares, "Who shall separate us from the love of Christ? Shall trouble or hardship or persecution or famine or nakedness or danger or sword?"

I was running from God. He was NOT running nor will he ever run away from me. I thought I knew what was best for me, but through my mess, God never left me. He always knew what I would get myself in and made a way for me to survive to testify to his goodness and mercy. I know that if God can rescue me from the smudge of this earth's perverted behavior, he can rescue you too. I left church that day feeling much better. I wasn't thinking about my behaviors. All I knew was I had a new beginning. Now maybe I could stop reading these magazines and maybe ask Sue to marry me.

How great was this! How great is my God! I loved this church. Soon after my conversion, I was baptized with my soon-to-be bride, although she didn't know it at the time. Every chance I had, I was in church. I had flashbacks of my grandpa's church and how, during the summers, we would go to the campgrounds and listen to different preachers. Everything was like camping. My relationship with God was influenced by the lifestyle of my grandparents as a child. Now here I was being influenced by another grandparent, Sue's grandma.

As I left church that day, I was excited about tossing out

the magazines, although I had to somehow get them out of my room to throw them away. However, I made a big mistake. My intentions were genuine, but once again I allowed myself to gaze at one of the magazines. I surrendered to my desires rather than remembering my experience with Christ. In my heart, I knew what I should have done, but this other voice was telling me it wouldn't hurt anything. Besides, God would forgive me. I fell for the lie.

## Competing Voices

The voice said: "Do you really want to throw away those great magazines? If you do, then it will cost you to buy more. Don't worry about what you did in church. It's true. You can still have those magazines and go to heaven."

That part was true. Nothing could stop me from going to heaven. But I decided I would just keep the magazines hidden and read them occasionally. I didn't have to do what they said. I would just read them and laugh. Satan never mentioned the feelings I would have every time I picked one up. He always had an answer. I went to church regularly, was learning from the Bible, memorizing verses, and falling more in love with Sue and her family.

My friends from church would say, "If your heart's not in it or you make up your mind to live two separate lives, stop! It won't work." The child of God must make up his mind. Who do you want to follow? The Lord or Satan? God will not force you to love him and live for him. It was me that decided to listen to Satan and do as he suggested. Nobody made me. God never makes his children obey or disobey, but disobedience to God is always the wrong choice. It's not the sinner God hates; it's the sin. It's the sin that keeps you out of heaven, not you. Because God loved me, I kept that as an excuse to sexually sin against him.

I soon learned how to use my adult magazines to get a thrill. I told myself I would never let what I read in the magazines get beyond what I could handle, but the more I read, the more I felt things changing inside. It seemed like a sport, a fun thing to do where nobody got hurt. I accepted my way of thinking, but I wouldn't take my consequences seriously, at least not right away.

Then I began to have the "I don't care" attitude. I figured since I was a child of God, if he didn't like what I was doing, then he should take it away. One voice would say, "Wow! Isn't she hot? Wouldn't you like to have her? Just think what you two would do. Relax and close your eyes. Now just picture you two together. See how it makes you feel. What a feeling, right? Who are you hurting? So what if God can see you if you're not hurting anyone. You're not married. You can have all the fun you want until you get married. Now sit back and enjoy the fantasy."

I believe that many of you can hear this voice telling you to think the same thoughts. I see this voice being played out in our culture. Nothing changes with Satan. The same old lies, the same old strategies. If his strategies work, he will continue to use them. The worst thing about him doing this is he attacks the church, the believers in Christ. How sad when we Christians listen to his lies. So, now I was listening to both voices, the one that said partake of the sin and the one that said to confess my sin.

Within two weeks, I returned to enjoying my magazines. Each time the desires would grow more intense and more frequent. When I was with Sue or in church, I would feel guilty, even miserable at times. One day, when I was alone with her, I asked her to marry me. She said yes.

## Engaged, Enlisted, and Gone

But what did I do? I went back to reading vulgar books and magazines. My life was going in so many directions. So many voices, so many thoughts. The convictions were wearing me out. I knew that what I was doing I shouldn't be, but I didn't care. Who was I hurting?

A bar was situated across the street from where I worked. Every time my friend Bob and I saw this place, we would tell each other how we couldn't wait until we hit twenty-one so we could drink in the bars. We were planning to have a party after we all hit that age. One day Bob was talking casually about the war, sharing that he wanted to get away from working with his dad. "I have been thinking about joining the army," he said, "but I don't know what I would do. I must get away from all this. All our friends are there. I feel guilty not going. I'm thinking I might check it out."

"I feel the same way, but I have a girlfriend. She would be very upset. I don't want to lose her. You want to join on a buddy system?" I offered.

"What's a buddy system?"

"It's where we join together and go through boot camp together."

"Let me think about it."

As that conversation mulled in our minds, I maintained my same routine of polluting my mind with more magazines but still was attending church. I harbored a desire to experience what I was reading, so I turned once again to the advertisements at the end of the magazines. With the full intention of carrying out acts I had seen in my magazines, I made a few calls. I wanted to experience the type of lifestyle I was reading about. My life was changing for the worse by the day.

Then the other voice spoke in my ear: *You shouldn't be doing this. You will regret it.*

*But I can't stop doing it. I love what I'm reading. I desire these women. They make me feel different. It makes me feel like I'm with them.*

It was February 1970 when Bob and I agreed to join the army in June. I had to tell Sue what I was going to do. After Vietnam, I would have to choose either to reenlist and have Sue join me or to get out. I was about to begin a whole new life. I knew I would have to throw away my magazines.

I would marry her after I got back, but for now, I couldn't drum up enough courage to tell her that I wanted to enlist. I didn't say anything to her about it for a month. How could I? I couldn't be certain whether I would even come back alive.

My thoughts were so scattered. *What am I thinking? Isn't this what I was trying to avoid? I don't have to join. I won't get drafted, but I could get away and start over. Maybe this is what I need. I will have time to think about my life. But I love Sue. I might lose her.*

Spending more time with Sue meant less time with my parents. I told my mom about how I wanted to join. She said the same thing I was thinking, but my dad hardly said a word at all about it; he just kept his thoughts to himself. Never a compliment or a supporting statement from my dad. As always, he would never change. I would get away from him too.

The closer we got to June, the more Bob and I tried to

convince ourselves not to go, but that changed when we both signed on the dotted line, joining the service. We were to be in Chicago on June 21, 1970. Sue graduated in May, but I ruined it by telling her that I had joined the army. I tried to console her by promising to return and marry her, saying she would be with me forever.

She replied, "What am I to do in the meantime? Just sit and wait? What if you die and never come back? What then? If you really love me, you won't go."

"It's too late, Sue. Bob and I already joined."

"You mean you did this without talking to me? How could you do this to me!" She then burst into tears.

"I need to get away. All my buddies joined. It's not fair to them if I don't serve too. I will be back home before I go to Vietnam. I will be gone for only ninety days."

"When do you leave?"

"June 21st."

"That's only a month away! That doesn't give us much time to be together," she said, tears streaming down her face.

"You'll be all right. Just keep going to church and stay here. You can write, and I'll call you every weekend. I will put you as my beneficiary, in case something happens to me."

"How can you do this to me, Bob? I can't sit here wondering if you're dead or alive. I thought we would be together without the military. I guess I was wrong. You went behind my back."

"I won't abandon you, Sue. I will send money and write to you. I need to serve my country. That's the least I can do. If I stay in, you can join me and we can start a family together. The government will pay for it. Don't be upset. Look at the good side of this."

"There is no good side if you're dead," she said, resigned.

I didn't know what to say after this. I knew I was wrong for not talking to her first. I was scared that I was going to lose her. I begged her to be patient and assured her everything would work out fine.

I threw my secret magazines in the trash when I walked away; I felt great. *This is the right thing to do, Lord, right? Please help me to overcome this habit. I love Sue, so I choose her over my habits. I know that what I am doing is wrong. I am so sorry that I even picked them up.*

Bob and I tried to continue working as if everything were normal. We were excited to join the army but also terrified. The day was rapidly approaching. Three more weeks and we would say goodbye to our jobs, this town, and whatever else we were running from.

I decided I would work in supply, and Bob wanted to be an infantryman. At least, I thought, I had a better chance of surviving than he did.

The time came, June 21st. I told Sue I would call her when I got to Chicago. My mom, dad, Sue, her mom, along with Bob and his dad were there to see us off, to say goodbye. As Bob and I boarded the train, I could see Sue crying as the train pulled away from the station. I doubted myself as I saw them disappear. *Would I ever see them again? Had I done the right thing?*

## Train Bound for a Change

As the train left them in the distance, I felt all alone. Everything I had, good and bad, I was leaving behind. I couldn't change my mind. I was ready for my next chapter. I wondered what would happen with Sue. Was she going to leave me? It was kind of late now for those kinds of thoughts.

After the train arrived in Chicago a few hours later, Bob and I walked to the YMCA and checked into our rooms for the night. Sitting on my bed at the YMCA, I thought back over the last five years. Though I was relieved because I had my diploma, I knew I didn't deserve it. I hadn't earned it. It was like a favor given to my mom. Here I sat now, independent. I was alone with no mom to help. No dad to ridicule me. No sporting events. *The fun is gone. Now comes my real test. I'm so scared. I just want to run back home. I just want to say I'm sorry and start all over again.*

For the next three months, I had no adult magazines. Basic training and AIT would take up most of my time. The YMCA was located next to the subway in Chicago. How people slept with the windows shaking every time it passed, I'll never know. All I know is there were no TV, radio, or magazines in the room, but there was one book in a drawer. It was the Gideon Bible.

I opened it and began to read. I remembered some of the verses I had heard the preacher mention in his sermons. Then I thought about church—the basement where Sunday school was held, the colored cross, and my mom who made us go. I felt guilty for the way I had disrespected God's house.

The next day, military personnel picked us up and took us to the main regional recruiting center, where we underwent a physical and took the oath to defend this country and the Constitution. That was a significant moment in my life that meant a lot to me. Before we took the oath, the captain gave us a chance to leave. I wanted to but didn't. After I took the oath, we were given a voucher, which guaranteed a one-way ticket to Ft. Lewis, Washington. I would be assigned to A-5-

2. Alpha company, here I come! I wanted to cry at the airport because what I had left behind at home rushed over me like a tidal wave. Suddenly, I realized life really wasn't that bad at home.

Approaching the Delta aircraft, I reminded myself that I had never flown on an airplane, and fear tagged into sorrow. Even though all the guys that were sworn in alongside of me were now on the same plane, my heart remained empty as the plane jetted down the runway. *Why was I thinking this way? Was I guilty of something? Had I made a mistake by doing this?*

Thirty-thousand feet above a nearly invisible earth, I yearned to reverse the plane and my life to go back and start over again. Thankfully, I soon fell asleep. Next thing I heard was, "Fasten your belt. We're about to land."

Around midnight, we got on the bus to Fort Lewis. I was looking forward to settling into our barracks, getting a good night's rest, and finding our military clothes in the morning. That's what normal people did. But the army wasn't normal. We were about to grow up fast. We were told that after completing our training here at Ft. Lewis, we would be sent off to Vietnam. I guess it was my turn now. I had a 50% chance of ever coming back.

## Unchangeable Memories

I was about to find out what this "free will" to choose meant—the choice that God gives us. I was going to learn what this Christian process meant. It would be later in my life before I truly understood what process had to do with Christians.

## Six

# Life in the Military

"This is not normal."

As the bus arrived, no sooner had the driver shut off the engine than some guy was screaming and swearing at the top of his lungs.

"Get off the bus, you maggots! I don't give a [bleep] how you get off! Through the windows, I don't give a [bleep]!"

The sound of that voice scared me to death. I stumbled off that bus as quickly as I could, almost falling. It didn't take me long to recognize that this madman was the head drill sergeant.

"Listen here, you sissy mama's boy. Get your [bleep bleep] in line! Do you know how to do that, or do I need to put a boot up your butt and show you?" Continuing his tirade, he mocked, "Oh boy, this is going to be fun with these little boys!"

He got in my face and asked me why I was laughing. "So, you think I have something on my face. Does it look like I do? If you think it's so funny, get down and give me twenty!"

I didn't know what that meant until he told another soldier to get down and do twenty. I thought, *Do twenty? I can't do ten.*

There it began, over a short period of time, that the drill sergeant adopted many names for me, none of which were nice, but soon I accepted them all and moved on. We never did go straight to our barracks. Instead, we were handed our military clothes, and we put them in our duffel bags. Then we marched to the barber shop to get our one and only free haircut, the buzz. From one place to another we marched. One guy said to me, "Sure, we get paid, but where does the army send your dead body when you come back from the war?"

"Dead? Who said anything about dying? Do you know something I don't? I don't want my mom to see me dead," I told the guy behind me.

"Think about it this way"—he shrugged—"just hope you die quickly. Who wants to come home with only one leg?"

"Me! I would rather come back alive and breathing than dead in a body bag."

We finally arrived at our barracks around five a.m., after our drill sergeant showed us how to make our beds. If a quarter didn't bounce on our beds, the drill sergeant tore the bed apart. Our bunks were to be kept made unless we were sleeping on them.

Our lives were in the hands of the three drill sergeants, whom I despised while I was going through boot camp. I had never experienced so much yelling in my life. Many times, I had to wipe another man's spit off my face, something I would have never accepted back at home. But here, I had to take it. If I resisted, I would have had to clean the barracks or the latrine with a toothbrush or wax the floors. At Fort Lewis, we were taught how to survive, how to shine our boots, and how to look presentable. Still, every day I missed Sue so much, my heart ached for her.

## Dear John

We often got letters or packages from home or the Salvation Army. I was three weeks into training when I received a letter from Sue. *Dear Bob* . . .

I had heard about the Dear John letters, but I never thought I would get one. As I opened the letter, I saw her engagement ring shining on that sorrowful piece of paper. My heart sunk. I was going to lose her because I had left. *I should have stayed.* The letter made me want to go AWOL. I wanted to go home.

I had to get to a phone, but they were all being used by the time I found them. All I could think about was her dating someone else. *Nothing good happens to me.* Finally getting a turn on the phone, I called Sue. When she answered, I spoke quickly. "Sue, I can only talk for fifteen minutes. What's wrong?"

"I can't sit here wondering if you're OK. I'm scared you might die over there," she confessed.

"You don't need to worry. When I finish, we can be together. Please don't do this. I don't think I can go through this without you. I only have two more months, and I'll be home for two weeks. We can talk about it when I get back home. Are you seeing someone else?" *Please say no. Please say no.*

"NO!"

*Thank God!*

"I'm just scared. I don't want to see you dead."

"If I decide to reenlist, you can come and live with me. We can see the world together. You know I love you. You're not the only one going through this. I don't want your engagement ring back. I want you to put it back on your finger.

Can you be patient till I come back home? I promise to call you every weekend."

"I hear what you're saying. I'm just scared I'll lose you. Send the ring back, and I'll put it back on. I miss having you around. My dad is driving Mom crazy. Grandma likes you a lot. She'll keep me busy in church. I do love you, Bob."

*Whew!* "I love you too." After I hung up the phone, I turned on my little radio, which was playing the Jackson Five's single, "I'll Be There." Every time I hear that song, it reminds me of that Dear John letter from Sue and my two long months in boot camp.

## Boot Camp

Arriving back at the barracks, the guys were waxing the floor. I never saw a place so shiny. You never crossed the drill sergeants. I made it a point to never look in their eyes. Eye contact meant you had their attention, and I never wanted to draw their attention.

Unfortunately, other guys did, and when *they* got into trouble, *we* all had to do extra duty. We were taught to cover each other's backs. And regarding the training, I didn't mind the walks, but running wasn't my expertise. An ambulance always followed us throughout our runs. If you fell back behind the ambulance, it picked you up. Twice it almost happened to me, but when I saw it getting closer, I pushed myself to finish the run. If you caught a ride with the ambulance, the name calling and belittling were terrible enough to make you believe what they were telling you was the truth.

One Sunday after chapel service while marching to the mess hall, I could smell the savory chicken awaiting us for dinner. *Finally, a good meal.* I could barely keep from running toward the chow line. As I took my first bite, I heard this unbelievable noise from the drill sergeants' table.

"I'm trying to eat over here! You maggots are smelling up this room. Now get your smelly [bleep] out of my sight! Go back and get ready for inspection!"

*Are you serious, you [bleep]!* I was thinking. *You mean to tell me that all this is going to waste. What about our Sunday noon meal, you good for nothing [bleep]!*

We didn't see the drill sergeants for about three hours. When we did, all three drill sergeants showed up. We were angry, hungry soldiers. We couldn't understand that they were making soldiers out of us so we would have a chance to come back alive from Vietnam.

After two more months of it, Bob and I graduated from boot camp. At our graduating party, the drill sergeants didn't act the same as they had during our training. They now treated us with respect. Only three guys didn't make it through boot camp, but Bob and I did. Dressed up in our dress greens, we went back to the barracks to wait for orders for our next assignment. I received mine the same day: I would train for my MOS at Atlanta Army Depot. First, though, I returned home for two weeks.

## Familiar Faces and Feelings

Landing at South Bend, Indiana, regional airport, I saw Sue waiting for her soldier. We ran toward each other, hugging and kissing the minute we met. The first thing I looked for was my ring on her finger. *Thank God, it's still there.* We planned to get married prior to my going to Vietnam. This way, she would be my spouse if something were to happen to me. She promised to keep busy while I was away, and I promised to call her every weekend. I spent most of my time with Sue. When I went to my family's home, my dad would continue to criticize me, so my visits were usually short.

I said goodbye to Sue and my family, then boarded the plane going to Atlanta. After the plane landed in Atlanta, I took a cab to the depot. I reported to the first sergeant, who assigned me my bunk. This assignment lasted for three months.

I don't remember much about that assignment, except for going downtown to Peachtree Street, which at that time was a red-light district. A group of us went to this strip bar. I was twenty-one, and this would mark my first visit to one of those places. And that's all it took. One time.

The memories of books and magazines flooded my mind as if I had never thrown them away. The next day I was thinking, *You know you want to go back down to those strip clubs. Think about last night when you went downtown. Weren't those girls hot? You have a three-day pass. Have a good time with the guys, but then go into a private room for viewing. It's better than the magazines, and now you can have both.* Instead of seeing still pictures of girls in magazines, I was staring at them in real life, in motion, within arm's reach, right in front of me. The guys were laughing and having a great time, but I was battling a heavy dose of guilt.

*Isn't this what I wanted? Wow! I like this, but I still feel like I'm cheating on Sue. But I'm not touching, just looking.* The familiar battle of the voices inside of my head had returned.

I noticed a sign on the wall that read: Ladies Night Out on Tuesdays. All Drinks Free. All Nude Male Dancers. Trying to justify my actions, I thought, *I bet Sue would go if she could. I wouldn't be jealous if she did. Well, maybe a little.*

I became very crafty at assuming someone's thoughts and actions. Assuming usually gets people into trouble. It did that night for me. I had let my guard down once again, and now I was back in the dark world of pornography. I had been counting the days to turning twenty-one for years, wanting to be able to go to bars, drink alcohol, look at nude dancers, and shop adult stores. Yet, in this familiar place, I thought I had buried my past. I began feeling convicted once again. This time the convictions were more intense. I really didn't want to do this, to be that person again, so why did I continue down the dark past?

"Oh yes, you wanted to," I felt that voice say once again. "You let yourself be open. Nobody made you come in here. This displeases the Lord. He knows the battle you're going through. It will only get worse unless you're willing to give it up. God won't make you choose. But if you continue to choose this lifestyle, there will be more consequences."

*Make these thoughts go away then*, I responded internally. *I don't ask for them to come into my head. They just appear. I'm just having a good time.*

That was true. We never ask for impure thoughts to come in our heads. The biggest, most powerful problem I had was my thoughts. I hated what was going through my head, and I hated it even more when I acted on them. I always knew that immorality was evil. I knew the magazines were a way to get my feelings and my body to react. Being in a nude dancers bar was different. I was now up close to what I had been reading and dreaming about.

I soon found out how those women teased men to get

money from them, but I was a tightwad. I wouldn't let them take my money. I would sit up front with my buddies looking up at these girls. I remembered what that voice said about the consequences.

*They are so pretty. All I'm doing is having fun and drinking with my friends. I'm not causing anyone problems.*
*What about Sue at home?*
*You had to bring her up. I won't tell her that I'm here. I'll keep it a secret.*
*You may keep it a secret from her, but you can't from the Lord. He sees all that you are doing.*
*Then tell him to stop these thoughts in my mind!* I wrestled.

The scripture in 1 Timothy 5:24 (ESV) reveals, "The sins of some people are conspicuous, going before them to judgment, but the sins of others appear later." There was something very different about the Holy Spirit. I didn't understand what was happening with these voices in my head, but the Lord allowed them. Yet, through it all, I learned who this God was. But it didn't matter sitting there at a bar in the depths of my darkness. I wanted him to leave me alone.

I wanted a God to let me live on my own terms. I would visit him on Sundays—that would be enough—but I hardly ever went to chapel services because I felt so guilty. The guys went from the bar to the street to hook up with prostitutes, but I had my limits. I wouldn't do that, although I did stop by the adult bookstore for some magazines.

*At least I'm not doing what they're doing*, I justified. I took the magazines back to my barracks, laid on my bunk, and fantasized about the women in them. *Oh, no! Now look what I've done. I shouldn't have bought these magazines. Oh well, nobody here. Just me and my magazines. Maybe I should have gone with the guys.*

Knowing about the strip club, so convenient and enticing, I ended up spending more and more time there. I knew it was wrong to go down there, but the attraction was overpowering. Something about that place kept drawing me. Meanwhile, my conscience kept visiting me.

Christians are not exempt from sexual temptations. Satan knows our weakness. He knows that if he can keep reminding us of our addictions, he can keep us weak and continuing in sexual sins.

Satan (afterward): "Now look what you did, and you call yourself a Christian. Where was your God? Now your God is going to pay you back for what you did. You'll be back because you're hooked. You know you like it. You can't stop. This is your world, the world of pleasure."

That's exactly what I thought. I couldn't stop because I didn't want to. I knew it was wrong, but I continued going down that road. The further I went, the more I wanted. Nothing was satisfying me.

## Preparing for Battle

The three months in Atlanta went by fast. My next assignment was Fort Lee, Virginia, where I had to take a quartermaster class, which kept me on base most of the time. Here it was easier to take a break from my magazines.

Vietnam loomed in my head as I took combat training at Fort Lee, so I decided to take my life more seriously. The training was intense. We learned about the traps the VC used, got shot by BB guns, went through an exploding made-up village, and experienced a surprise attack by UH1 choppers. Was I scared? I think all of us were.

After this training, I wondered if I would die. Before

going to my last stop prior to Vietnam, APO San Francisco, I was given a pass to go home for one week. That week was sad for Sue. She knew that I had a 50% chance of coming back home, and we put off getting married until I returned.

Still, I spent most of my time with her, although I did visit my parents. Mom wept. Dad criticized. *Just one time, can't you be proud of me? Why do you have to be so stupid?* I gave my mom a hug and kiss, and said goodbye.

Here we were once again, at the airport. I said my goodbyes. As the aircraft ascended, the last thing I saw was the Golden Dome of my favorite university, Notre Dame, home of my favorite team.

## Detours

We changed planes at O'Hare and then headed nonstop to the bay. After landing, three other soldiers and I heading to the same place hailed a taxi, gave the driver our vouchers, and headed to the APO quarantine unit. There we checked in and were given our M-16s, a gas mask, and our orders to Saigon, Vietnam.

Nothing else to do but wait. Every so often over the loudspeaker we heard platoons being ordered to fall in and saw them standing in front of their aircraft. Two days went by until finally I heard our platoon being called. I grabbed my weapon, mask, and duffel bag, and fell in.

I was ready, prepared to join my fellow soldiers in Vietnam. Then, I heard the captain calling names to fall out and wait for other orders. Hoping on one hand to hear my name and the other hand not, I listened and heard, "Private Gushwa." As I looked at the C130 closing its doors behind the last soldier, I felt relieved for my life being spared, but also felt like I was betraying my buddies in Nam. Then, I became bitter.

## All This Training for Nothing

I was willing to trade places with other soldiers, but when I tried, my first sergeant thought I was crazy. After being transferred to a general population barracks with other guys waiting for other orders, I called Sue and gave her the good news. I had never before heard anybody crying and screaming at the same time.

The first sergeant asked if I wanted a thirty-day pass before going to Germany. If I did, I would be fifteen days over for the next year. I said yes. In the next hour, I had my orders to report to the $71^{st}$ reporting company in Frankfurt, Germany, where I would be given another set of orders to be assigned for the next thirty-six months.

I grabbed a cab the next day and flew back to South Bend, Indiana, where Notre Dame's Golden Dome welcomed me home. I was happy to see Sue but angry at the army for betraying me. I had joined to defend my country and honor my fellow soldiers. That anger would stay with me even after my release from the army.

Standing in front of Sue, I could tell there was something pressing on her mind. She waited until we were alone to tell me that she was pregnant.

*That's why I didn't go to Vietnam. God, you knew Sue was pregnant. You knew my place was here. But we're not married. We need to get married.*

We talked to our pastor about baptizing us both at the same time because I hadn't ever been baptized. Then we sat down with counseling from the pastor to plan our wedding. It would be in our church. I wore my dress greens, and Sue looked beautiful. The wedding went well. Everything I said to her, I meant from the heart.

My full intentions were to be a good husband to her and a father to our child. With her only being eight weeks pregnant, things would surely work in our favor for beginning our family life together. Or so I thought.

Fortunately, at the wedding reception my dad acted civilized and at least he was in a church. Within a month, I had been detoured into missing the plane going to Nam, told I was going to be a father, and been married to the mother of my child. Nevertheless, it was now time for me, PV2 Gushwa, to leave for Germany. I told Sue all I needed was one more rank, and then she could come to Germany where we would live off base.

Once again, I boarded the plane alone, but this time I hoped it was for the last time. The next time would be my wife moving to Germany. A charter flight from Chicago's O'Hare landed me in Frankfurt, Germany.

After I landed, a bus took some of us soldiers to an old WWII POW Camp. Only one section was used by American soldiers, but I had a chance to tour the other side and see where they kept enemy soldiers chained up. It was like a dungeon in the ground. Many men died there. I never went back to that dungeon.

# Seven

# Kaiserslautern, Germany

Within a week, I had my orders to report to Kleber Kaserne in Kaiserslautern, Germany. A busload of us took the three-hour trip. Once we arrived, we were given barrack assignments, ate dinner, and then settled into our barracks. The military does not waste time.

The next day we fell in and were given our assignments. Inside Kleber Kaserne was the Army Depot. It was the dumping ground for WWII trucks, jeeps, and other vehicles. Inside the main building were wooden crates of M1s and M14s. My job was to account for all weapons and ammunition, handwriting the inventory once a week.

My second day in Germany, I noticed a chapel just outside the Kaserne called Kleber Chapel. Assigned to the chapel was a chaplain I came to appreciate. He often sat behind his desk playing his banjo. It was here where I perfected my game of playing both sides. I would go to church, stay married, commit adultery, and use the prostitutes. Figuring out how to devise a plan not to get caught was an ongoing challenge.

One afternoon, our squad was permitted a pass for the afternoon. I thought I would check out the chapel because I needed a place to take Sue when she came to Germany. I hesitated to enter the doorway. In my heart, I knew I was deliberately sinning against God. I had managed to once again get adult magazines, and in Europe, prostitution was legal.

Setting my guilt aside, I headed in the sanctuary and instantly fell in love with what I was seeing. A chaplain's assistant greeted me, and then he introduced me to the chaplain. Though he was a major, he did not act superior like others in his rank. Volunteers worked in the chapel, who appeared to be spouses of officers and NCOs. In the chapel, rank didn't matter when worshiping. I never once saw the chaplain use his rank on someone. He was a man for God, serving both God and country. Many times during the church service, he would play the banjo and sing with his wife. He also invited musical guests who were touring military bases. Every chance I could get, I stole away to the chapel, learning about the chaplain's assistant job. I had decided I wanted to be one and change my MOS to "chaplain's assistant."

I privately talked to the chaplain about being able to work in the chapel and apply for the MOS. He talked with my company commander, and because my current MOS was overstaffed, my captain allowed me to work in the chapel. One of the chaplain's assistants was transferred to another assignment, and I was soon able to fill his slot.

When life stresses us out, sometimes we give up on God. I hated what I was doing with my life, and I loved being able to serve as a chaplain assistant. Still, I didn't want to quit my secret life regardless of how badly I wanted to.

*What is it that keeps me wanting to look at these pictures? Now I want to experience what it would be like to be with a prostitute. Stop thinking that way! You work in the chapel. You're about to bring your family here.*

*Do you want to get caught? But I know I wouldn't get*

*caught. I will keep my porno magazines in my briefcase under a lock. Nobody will know. I will be friends with my buddies in the barracks and still have friends in the chapel.*

So, there it began. Living two lives. Was I the only one who had this problem?

I knew I needed to talk to someone about my addiction, but I felt that they might think I was unfit to serve in the military. At the barracks, I was "one of the guys," but at the chapel, I was a saint in the eyes of the chaplains and the churchgoers. I might have fooled those people, but I knew in my heart that I wasn't fooling God.

One Saturday night, some of the guys in the barracks planned to go out on the town, so I tagged along. They went to this local bar where Americans hung out to find young women. Sooner or later, the guys found women to hook up with. I had my chance but didn't want to be seen by someone who attended the chapel, so I went back to the barracks and pulled out my magazines instead. On my bunk I lay pouting. I'd had a chance to experience a prostitute but hadn't taken it.

Later the guys came back drunk, telling me about their dates just to get me upset. It worked. Once the guys told me where to pick up the hookers, I knew I had to get a car so I could do what I wanted without needing anyone else to know about it. I heard about a guy living in the barracks who wanted to sell his car because he was getting out of the army and going back home. I was approved for a loan with the credit union and bought his car. Now I had a chance to pick up women at the bar.

I felt great because I had a car, worked in the chapel, and could enjoy my pornographic magazines in secret. The next month I was promoted to PFC ranking, which enabled me to live off base with my wife. I couldn't live on base until I had four years in and an E4 ranking. I was excited about bringing Sue to Germany, and I was determined to give up my nasty habit. I needed to do this for Sue. I needed to be an example for my son as he grew older.

After my promotion, I requested a housing allowance and a separate rations allowance for food. After another month, my request was approved. When I started receiving the allowance, I looked for an apartment. I found one where we could live upstairs, while the landlord lived downstairs. A couple from Alabama, with whom we soon became friends, would later fill the other empty apartment.

The day arrived for me to drive to Frankfurt and pick up Sue. She had never flown in her life, so I was looking forward to asking her how it had gone. I stood waiting for her to get off the aircraft, thinking, *There she is, my pregnant wife, carrying my son, who will be born in Germany.* I was the luckiest guy in the world. Married, working at the chapel, I met great friends and learned much from them, especially about being a Christian.

One Pentecostal friend I knew, Roger, always praised the Lord, no matter what, even when he hit his thumb with a hammer. "Ouch, ouch, ouch. Praise the Lord!"

"Praise the Lord for what?" I asked.

"For me hitting my thumb with a hammer."

"Are you out of your mind? So, you hit your thumb with a hammer. Does it hurt?"

"Of course. But instead of swearing about it, I thank the Lord."

"Oh yeah? Let me get this straight. Thank you, God, for this pain. It really feels good. Look God, I'm bleeding. But thank you anyway. Are you crazy?"

"No. Just giving God all the praise for everything in my life."

"Geez, Roger, get a life."

But he did have a life. A life with Christ. Something I needed and knew about but wouldn't give up everything for. Unlike him, I always tried to compromise with God.

## A New Birth

One Sunday night, Roger invited me to attend a local Pentecostal church. I kind of enjoyed it but then came the preaching—hell, fire, and brimstone. What came next was even more surprising. People started speaking some weird language. Roger turned to me (possibly because of the look on my face) and asked, "Do you speak in tongues?"

"No! But I'm trying to learn the German language."

"I'm talking about being filled with the Holy Ghost and speaking in a spiritual tongue."

I was confused. It was enough I was tempted to give in to my sexual bad habits and now this tongue stuff. What did I have to do to make God happy? It seemed like no matter what I did, I was unhappy.

A certain hill was situated near where I lived. I figured if Moses could climb a mountain, then I could climb this hill. One Sunday afternoon, I climbed that hill. I knelt there on my knees full of conviction because I knew I was disobeying God. I begged him to take this habit away from me. He is God, after all! I knelt there on that hill in tears, begging God. I was helpless trying to get rid of this burden.

I knew I couldn't negotiate with God, but I could promise him something: *God, if you would just take these thoughts from my head, I will throw the magazines away.*

I was serious because more than anything, I didn't want to lose my family. The guilty convictions were tearing me up every time I was around my Christian friends, not that they were intentionally putting guilt on me. This wasn't a bad thing, but simply being around them brought a different sense of who I should be.

I walked back down that hill, serious about changing. At the chapel, some of us formed a new group called the young married group. The purpose of our group was to help young married couples get back and forth from the commissary, doctors, and laundry; however, we didn't have a proper vehicle, which would be a problem for anyone trying to transport others from point A to point B. I did what I could with my one car, but we needed a van. A lieutenant colonel who attended the chapel helped us get a VW Bus. The guys took turns driving, and our group grew under the support of Chaplain Hunt and our church.

During the time I served in that chapel, there were only three services in the chapel—Jewish, Catholic, and Protestant. Talking about Jesus was never discouraged. Invitations to accept Christ were always encouraged. The military has certainly changed since then. What a shame! Our chapel was given a grant to open a coffee house where troops could go to have a good time, listen to music, and play games. At our coffee house, Christians would also share their faith with the military.

Thanks to the Lord and Chaplain Hunt, we now had a young married group with a coffee house. Back at the apartment, a friend named Cecil and I liked to invite the young married couples over occasionally. Since I had the car, the four of us traveled around Germany. Cecil and I had one

## Kaiserslautern, Germany

thing in common—both our wives were pregnant.

One day at work, I received a call that Sue was in labor. Before I could get there, the ambulance had already taken her to Landstuhl Army Hospital. When I arrived at the hospital, the admissions desk informed me that Sue had been sent to labor and delivery. Before going to see her, I went back outside to get a fresh breath of air where I saw this old Red Cross, WWII-type vehicle. I asked the nurse if my wife had ridden in that. She said yes. Later, I would tell my son Mike about that vehicle.

I sat in the waiting room watching and listening to soldiers who were being flown in from Vietnam, and I was reminded instantly of families who would never be the same. Guilt began to weigh heavy on my mind because I felt like I should have been there with them. My name should have been called out. Then, I wondered how many had died without Christ.

While I was deep in thought, I heard the voice of Dr. Husbands saying, "PFC Gushwa."

"Yes."

"The delivery went well. Your wife and baby are doing fine. If you want to see them now, follow me."

When I walked into the room and saw Sue holding baby Mike, I felt so proud. Holding my newborn, Mike, I told God that I would be a good husband and father. I would never go back to my old ways. After three days in the hospital, I took Sue home to our apartment full of friends. Even our landlords, two of the sweetest people we had met, were there. They loved the Americans. They kept our rent cheap and constantly asked us if we needed anything. They became like grandparents to our child.

*It Only Takes One Look*

There I was living in Germany with a loving wife, a healthy son, supportive church friends, a good job, and loving landlords. Everything was going so great. We had Bible studies in the coffee house, which helped me grow spiritually. Everything I was learning was going to my mind and into my heart. After one of our studies, Roger walked up to me and asked, "Do you believe that God, Jesus Christ, and the Holy Spirit are one?"

"No! How can that be? On the cross, Jesus wasn't talking to himself. He was talking to God. So how could they be one and the same? They are three separate persons."

Roger believed differently. His faith annoyed me sometimes. He knew so much, and I knew so little, but I wanted to know much more. Roger confused me with his talk of speaking in tongues, the indwelling of the Holy Spirit, Jesus as everything. I didn't know what I believed. I only knew that Christ died for me. I remembered when I climbed that hill to be closer to God. I didn't want to climb that hill again because it was a steep hill to climb in the first place.

Out of frustration and confusion, I went to an empty room downstairs in the chapel. I knelt with my Bible open and said to the Lord: "Lord, I kneel before you because I don't understand you or the Bible. I know that you died on the cross, and yet I know very little. I don't understand how you can be one—God, Father, Holy Spirit. I don't understand all the tongues stuff, and I'm not going to praise you if I hit myself with a hammer. I kneel before you because I figure if you are God, you will teach me about yourself and give me clarity on what the Bible means. I don't trust anybody to tell me the truth anymore. So, I lay my Bible before you and ask that you tell me the truth. Take these sexual feelings away from me, or I will give in to them because I am weak. Please, Lord! Amen."

From that day on, the Lord kept his promise to me. He never told me how I was going to learn, nor how much I would go through. He never told me the burdens I would carry or the people I would hurt, but he promised to always be there for me. He kept his promise too.

Here I am alive, writing this story. I never thought I would reach this point in my life, but God has a way of leading us through the storm so that our testimony can be shared with others, to help others.

God has never fully told me why he allowed me to go through trials and fall into temptations. He always warned me upfront, always allowed me to make my own decisions, but through it all, I learned much about Christ. Still, the one thing we will never understand remains a mystery: Why does God allow so much wickedness to come in our lives? How could a loving God sit up there and watch us mess up and hurt other people?

There were answers, but it would take years for me to learn the truth. I would have to listen to the Holy Spirit and read God's Word. I had to talk to him a lot, and often his answers weren't quite what I expected. He would gently remind me in my times of doubt that his ways weren't mine.

*For my thoughts are not your thoughts, neither are your ways my ways, declares the Lord* (Isaiah 55:8).

When I left the chapel, I felt empty inside, waiting for something to fill it. Every time someone told me about their beliefs, I asked them where it was in the Bible. I used commentaries and the Bible to find the truth. I was filling my mind and heart with God's Word, often wondering how people lived in the Old Testament days.

## Back and Forth

One day I took Sue to Ramstein Air Force Base because I wanted to buy a Colt .45 pistol. I loved taking it to the shooting range. Sue was scared that Mike could get ahold of it, but I always kept it hidden. This innocent purchase would prove to be a nearly fatal moment in our lives.

Then it happened! One Sunday night after service, I took Mike and Sue back home. I told her I had forgotten something at the chapel, but instead I drove down to a place where the barracks guys said prostitutes could be found. As I drove around the block, two familiar voices were speaking to me.

Left Ear: "Take a look at her. Isn't she hot? You're never gonna know what it's like unless you try it. Nobody will know. Your wife's asleep. Nobody is here. Look, she is waving at you. Just go talk to her."

Right Ear: "If you listen to Satan, you will fail. Think of your wife asleep in bed; she trusts you. Do you want to lose that? It's your decision, but if you go through with it, then there will be consequences."

Nobody told me about getting these feelings when I saw these girls. If I would have just gone home that night, the guilt that would haunt me would never have happened. I took the bold move to say no to God. Nobody made me do it. I was fully responsible for the act I was about to do.

After I left that area, I felt miserable. I also never had this type of guilty feelings before. It was a different guilt. The same voice who tricked me was the same one condemning me. I felt dirty and filthy. It was hard to look at my wife and

## Kaiserslautern, Germany

child. The next day at work, I felt like I had betrayed the entire congregation. I began to blame God for not stopping Satan. *Why did you let him trick me? I felt like you set me up. This is not funny. What kind of a God would sit up there watching me do it? I don't want to live like this.*

Because I had fallen for the lie once again, considering myself a personal failure, I figured, *Why not look at pornography again? After all, I blew it, so what's the use? I will just have to keep my pictures under lock and key.* So, I once again went down to the PX and bought a nice carrying case with a combination and told Sue that I had papers I needed to carry with me. That case became my hiding space for all my adult books and magazines.

When I was alone, I opened the case and read my magazines. For two weeks, I was torn up inside;, but even then, I put up a front. I still read the Bible, talked to God, went to Bible studies, and attended church. I convinced myself that I could fool my family and friends, and sometimes, I guess, even God.

I still knew two guys who lived in the barracks who always chased the ladies on the weekends. I began to tag along with them, except for when they went to this one three-story building. I just couldn't go in. I knew it was an adult community center for the US troops. Guys drank, played pool, and did *other things.*

I never did go, but I was still tempted on the weekends. Playing back and forth, sinner and saint, was getting to me. I knew I was saved, but I didn't understand why God was allowing this to happen to me. I felt my wife needed someone better than me.

One night, I pulled out my Colt .45 and put bullets in the

chamber. I told Sue that I was going to end my life. I told her how guilty I felt for not going to Vietnam. That was true, but it was not the real reason I thought of taking my life. She cried out, "Please don't do this!"

Then, I saw my little boy walk in our room. I felt so convicted looking at him. I ran outside to cry, drove away, and then parked the car in a dark place where I cried. While in deep thought, I fell asleep until about one in the morning when I went home to a crying wife with my son lying next to her.

My heavy heart led me to my wife's side on the bed. "I am so sorry," I pleaded. I told her that I would sell the gun, the gun I loved so much. I would give up the gun for my family. The rest of the night, I just cuddled next to Sue, wondering how I could stop my secret lifestyle, still weighing if I should just keep it a secret. I never did go back out on the streets the rest of my tour in Germany, but I kept my magazines.

After two years in Germany, Sue and I decided to go home for thirty days. Prior to us going home, my friend Cecil's wife, Brenda, had her baby Blaine, who would become Mike's little buddy. Our thirty days went by fast. We stayed at my parents' house. Family visited us when my mom had a cookout. We visited our friends, and I went to a Notre Dame football game with my brother-in-law.

When we returned to Germany, Cecil and I had to go back to work. Heading down the hill from our apartment, my car, which used about a can of braking fluid every week, was supposed to stop at the bottom of the hill at the stoplight. Dressed in our fatigues, we got in the car, but I had forgotten something important when I got back from military leave: I

## Kaiserslautern, Germany

forgot to put brake fluid in the car. As we got closer to the stoplight I pressed on the brakes, but the pedal went all the way to the floor. We weren't slowing down. We were racing to the bottom.

"Oh no, Cecil! I forgot to put braking fluid in! I have no brakes!"

"Try using the emergency brake. I hope the train isn't coming. I'm going to jump."

"Hold on! Open your door and try stopping it with your boots."

And that's what we did. I pulled on the emergency brake as hard as I could and put my left leg out. We were lucky. The car stopped just in time. In shock, all we could do was laugh. When we checked our boots, we could see where the bottoms had been worn down.

On the way home from work, Cecil and I stopped to buy some haddock fish. Our wives tried to fry them for dinner. We sat down together to eat, but when we took one bite of the fish, we all started looking around the table at each other, Cecil saying, "Yuck! This is gross. It's pizza time." We had good times with friends in Germany. Even today, Cecil and I still talk about these two events.

My assignment to Germany was ending, and Cecil had decided to get out. I decided to reenlist, but this time I changed my MOS to chaplain's assistant. We knew that leaving Germany would leave behind many memories. I had spent thirty-six months jumping back and forth between right and wrong. When I received my new assignment, I hoped it would be the new beginning I needed.

Eight

# Fort Detrick, Maryland

I received my orders for a new assignment to Fort Detrick, located in Frederick, Maryland. When I arrived, I was jokingly told to hang up my uniform because, "This place is run by civilians." I knew they didn't mean that literally, but it was true. My chaplain was from the same denomination as me. Life seemed to change, but all it took was one small temptation and me to be foolish enough to listen and act on it.

Our first home was in a small town called Thurmont. We rented a single mobile home that sat on a concrete slab on top of a hill. One night a terrible storm came through and almost sent our mobile home tumbling down the hill, so I decided it was time to move closer to work.

We found a nice apartment closer to work, but staying put in that mobile home would have been much better for me. Next to our complex was a shopping center, and not too far from that shopping center was an adult bookstore. It seemed like everywhere I went, temptation was there.

I didn't have the strength to fight it, so I once again gave in and bought some magazines. It had been awhile since I bought magazines, so when I saw the new ones, I was shocked—more shocking photos, more ads to meet people, and, the most shocking of all, marriage was now "open."

## Fort Detrick Maryland

I always found ways to talk to women on the phone. I wanted to meet them but never could find the time nor the will. Every day when I read the newspaper, I went to the classified ads. I looked specifically for the housesitting ads, which I called, pretending that I needed someone to watch my home. I would keep it interesting by changing the subject about myself going on business trips. Then, I would manipulate the phone call by getting the woman on the other end of the phone line to tell me about her personal problems. Cell phones and computers were not yet invented for the home, so I had to use other phones.

When I wasn't busy, I would chat on the phone in the office too. Just like always, I kept this a secret. Step by step, day by day, I was learning to live an illicit lifestyle. I tried to fight off urges, and in most cases, it worked because I tried to keep busy. This was a dream assignment for me because few military uniforms were seen.

While stationed there, we had the opportunity to celebrate our nation's 200th birthday in Washington, DC. The pageantry was something to behold. Then, there was Watergate and the impeachment of President Nixon. I can still remember him waving to the crowd when he left the Oval Office. Things have changed in this country since then.

Our government seems to have never learned a lesson from its own corruption. Television programs have become more revealing, explicit, and inappropriate for families and children. Adult theaters were popping up everywhere, and I managed to go behind my wife's back to see what they were like.

At least for a while, I had figured out how to keep my guilty feelings in check. I blamed my behavior on my past, saying such things to myself as: *This is who I am. I tried to change, but I couldn't, so I give up. No use in trying when you can't stop it. I don't put these thoughts in my head, so why should I care?*

Our apartment home was close to Fort Detrick, and our friends were few in number. Our chapel too was very small, consisting mostly of older retired military and middle-aged soldiers. One Saturday afternoon, my chaplain called me to ask if I could do a Sunday morning service. Of course, I agreed, even though I was thinking, *Are you serious? I'm a struggling Christian with a sexual bad habit, and you want me to preach? I can't. Not with these magazines I have.*

So, what did I do? I drove home, took out my magazines, and threw them away, thinking that it would make me feel better, ease my conscience. I questioned God repeatedly. *Why?* The chaplain's son became very ill and there were no other chaplains close by, so I felt obligated to fill in. I was scared to death, though, because my convictions weighed heavy on my mind. I had a hard time preparing notes because of my convictions. I kept thinking, *I can't do this. I would be a hypocrite. I can't look at these people knowing that I'm a fake, but that's what I have become, a fake. I'm good at it. I can put on a mask and play preacher for forty minutes. My wife will be proud of me. My chaplain will think I am a great Christian, and God might look down on me differently because I would be trying to quit my habit.*

So, I stood up at the podium with my fake smile and presented a sermon about David. Yes, David. I figured he and I had a lot in common. We both sinned willingly against God, and we both covered our sin. Sue smiled up at me, and the people shouted, "Amen!"

## Fort Detrick Maryland

After the service, the people shook my hand and told me I'd done a great job. I cleaned up the chapel and went home with Sue. Later that day, my chaplain called and complimented me on a job well done. He put me in for a good conduct medal and a promotion. I received both and became a specialist 4. I was proud. One more rank and I would be an NCO.

For about six months, I was behaving as a good husband, but once again it didn't last when I drove by the adult bookstore. Satan always knew the best time to get my attention. It was night, and the lights on the billboard were flashing. I heard the voice again: "Look, Bob. Remember that place? Things have changed since the last time you were in there. Don't you want to just go in and look? You don't have to buy a magazine. There are new things in there, and they have bargains."

Of course, I went in and looked around, hoping no one would see me go in. Satan was right, the place had changed. Now there were live women behind a small window in a room. For 25 cents, the window went up, and you could see a woman dancing nude. Her job was to get you to use more quarters. Did it work?

When the temptation becomes overwhelming and you refuse to use the tools that God has given you to fight back, most likely you will give in. So, I did. However, I didn't have far to go home, which made it hard to take the guilt off my face by the time I had to be the "other me." When I walked in my home, Sue was giddy, while I was confused and guilty at the same time.

"Why are you so happy?" I asked.

"I am pregnant!"

"Is it a boy or a girl?"

"I don't know yet. I see the doctor on Monday. You need to come."

That evening, I told my chaplain the good news, and he and his wife visited us with flowers and congratulations. I didn't know why, but every time something good happened, I was always able to throw away my magazines. I was going to have two children. On Monday we found out that this baby would be a little girl. Little Mike was excited about having a sister to play with.

## Siblings

I wasn't allowed to go into the delivery room at that time, so Mike and I watched TV in the waiting room until the nurse came in and told me that I had a healthy baby girl. I woke Mike up to see his baby sister. He looked and then promptly fell asleep in the chair.

I was proud to have a family. When I was younger, I had dreamed of having a family, never imagining the happiness I would feel sitting in the hospital with my family. I also never dreamed I would ever have to deal with this addiction that interrupted my life at every turn.

Now Mike was a big brother. When Mike was a baby, he struggled with colic, but my new daughter was a great baby. Although Mike got jealous of his sister at times, he often got frustrated with her because he wanted her to grow up fast so she could play with him. We taught Mike how to feed her the bottle, which he wanted to do more often than she needed it. He thought feeding her more would make her grow faster.

What a life! I had it great, and for a little while, once again, I believed I had put my troubles behind me. That lasted until the day a young woman with a troubled marriage walked into my office. The chaplain was counseling a couple for marriage when I noticed that he gave them a marital test to assess the condition of their relationship.

After they took the test, he gave it to me to grade, using an answer sheet. As I read through the questions, my mind began to wander into a dreadful place, thinking, *I wonder how many people believe this stuff. Maybe I could use a test like this to trick women into thinking they have a hopeless marriage.*

As if my thoughts had not already sunk to a new low, I then noticed the woman's telephone number was on the information sheet. I was tempted to call her, making up an excuse to meet with her, to tell her how bad her marriage was and how the test proved it. Then, I would make a move on her, convincing her that I cared.

Even though I was married, it didn't matter. I was looking for other women. I convinced her to meet at her home. That's what I did. I knocked on her door, introducing myself as the chaplain's assistant. I acted like a nice guy who cared about her marriage. She had no kids, so I thought I had a chance.

Her husband was at work, so she and I were alone. It was a very dangerous situation to be in, but my emotions were taking over. Sue never entered my mind as I explained to the woman the test results I had invented. I told her that their marriage would never work because she and her husband weren't compatible. I tried to get her to believe she needed someone to care about her. I told her how I had seen so many marriages with husbands who didn't care about their wives. Persuading her like the voice in my head had so often done with me, I said, "Why should you stay in a marriage when all

## It Only Takes One Look

he does is work and drink with his friends? He is leaving you here all alone. That's not fair. How do you know he's not cheating on you? I bet he is! I have seen this before. You need to get out of this marriage. I just wanted to stop by and let you know. Give me a call if you're interested."

"OK, I will."

She called all right. She called my chaplain. I don't know what she said to him, but I recall what my chaplain said to me: "Chaplain's assistants are not allowed to visit the clients. You are not allowed to test anyone. Do we understand each other?"

"Yes, sir."

Since I got off the hook, I felt relieved and was thankful to never see her again. I wanted to tell Sue, in case the chaplain might mention it to her, but I kept quiet.

Soon thereafter, we got to see President Nixon wave at us in Thurmont, MD, when he landed at a football field, then drove off to Camp David. We spent a week touring, but when I got back to the office, on my desk were my orders. My orders stated that I would be assigned to the 559th artillery group in Vicenza, Italy.

I dropped like a lead balloon in my chair. Staring at my orders, a heavy weight once again fell in my heart and mind. I had gotten everything I wanted on my dream sheet, but there and now I had to make a decision that could change my world forever. I didn't have much time left in the army, so either I had to reenlist and go to Italy or get out.

*Here's my chance. I'm going to Italy. They are Catholics. They don't cheat or have prostitutes. They don't have adult bookstores. Thank you, Lord. Maybe now I can beat this.*

With excitement over the possibility of living free from

temptation, I arrived home to tell Sue about us going to Italy. Mike was five years old, so leaving in the summer worked out for his schooling. Before leaving for Italy, we took leave to see our families at home.

 We took the kids to see their grandparents, but I sensed an awkwardness on my side of the family among my siblings and, as always, with my dad. Mom was a great grandma, but my siblings seemed to ignore us. I couldn't hold a conversation with my dad because all he did was put me down in front of my family. My brother would egg him on, which made it worse for all of us.

When I mentioned what I had learned about the Lord, my brother mocked me. I ignored him by sitting alone in a room or taking a walk outside. Sue and I usually sat by ourselves until Mom would get us to play games.

My children didn't know who these people were. They were the first grandchildren born to the family, but that didn't seem to matter. Regardless of how we felt, we tried to be patient, putting up a front.

Visiting Sue's family was much more comfortable and peaceful for us. Her family was fun to be around. We laughed, shared stories, and played games. When I was around her family, I felt wanted. My mom disliked the fact that I enjoyed my in-laws more than my own family. I blamed it on my dad. Here I was serving my country in the army, now getting a chance to come home. The least he could do was respect the military. I thought he would be proud of me. *C'mon, Dad, give me hug,* I thought, but no, not even a handshake. Just a nod of the head, another cut down, with useless name calling. *Nothing ever changed.*

Dad never knew how much he hurt my feelings when he

called me names and disrespected me in my uniform. I never knew how much this would end up affecting me. Many times, when a parent puts down a child, it can affect them. *Would I someday be the same way as my dad?*

Since we rented a car from O'Hare, we could say our goodbyes from each of our parents' homes. We went to my home first to say goodbye. Mom hugged me, and when my dad shook my hand, I was shocked. Then we went back to Sue's family home, loaded our car, and said our goodbyes.

Sue's brother announced, "We're coming to Italy next summer to visit."

"You're seriously willing to fly for six hours? If you do, it's best to fly at night. That's what we're doing. The kids will sleep then. See you then. Bye."

# Nine

# Vicenza, Italy

After we arrived at our base, our family had to stay in temporary housing until they found off-base permanent housing. My assignment was not in a chapel. Although we had an office in the chapel, my job wasn't part of the chapel services. Instead, I was to support my chaplain by driving him to ten missile sites where he held services and visited the troops.

We visited the sites twice a month, so I was driving a lot of miles. Driving without an accident in Italy was considered a good job. Sue kept busy managing the Christian bookstore at the chapel. Our little Mike attended the American school on base, and we enrolled our daughter at a local Catholic school downtown where many American preschool kids attended.

I remember a time when Sue and I picked her up from school. She ran to us, speaking English even though the nuns told her to speak Italian in school, which she was learning to do there. We ended up taking our daughter out when she was able to go to the American school on base.

I thought I had been freed of my bad habit when I arrived in Italy. I hadn't expected the guys in our unit talking about their Italian weekend experiences. When the chaplain and I went to the missile sites, guys had pornography lying around.

## It Only Takes One Look

I asked them how they got the porn here in a Catholic country.

They just laughed and rolled their eyes. Upon hearing their source, I knew I would have to check it out. Something in me had no problem shopping the adult bookstores. Magazines were written in different languages, but I didn't care. It was the pictures I liked.

We received mail every day by going to the post office on base. I soon figured out how to get pornography sent to me in a white package. Just as before, I kept my magazines hidden in my briefcase. I brought my case with me every time the chaplain and I went down to the missile sites. Sometimes I sat in the car and looked at them.

I still managed to play the nice Christian man, though. Inside, however, I was full of lust for women. I found out how to speak the basics of Italian just to talk to the prostitutes. *But how can there be such women in a country full of Catholics? Oh well. I guess it doesn't matter if you're having a good time. I never could understand how there could be so much fun when there was so much pain inside on the way home. Now I have a wife and two children. How could I do this?*

At some point, while living this double life once again, now in Italy, I began to search for answers from the Bible. That didn't mean I would quit my habit; I just wanted to know why I was so hooked on my addiction, why I could not let go.

I never realized while I was in the thick of the mess that God was working his purpose in my life. This wouldn't be revealed to me until later. Worse consequences would finally grab my attention. Promoted to Specialist 5 and a proud

## Vicenza, Italy

member of the NCO Club, I felt important then. I was moving up in the ranks. Being stationed in Italy with a family and having close Christian friends is what I needed. I never had problems with transportation because before I left Fort Detrick, I bought a car and had it shipped to Italy. I had it refinanced by an American Credit Union on base, and we used it to travel throughout Italy, visiting Rome, Florence, Venice, and other places.

Seeing the ruins from New Testament times, such as Pompeii, was incredible. We took a chairlift to the top of Mt. Vesuvius, where we could see smoke from an active volcano. I also learned to speak their language enough to shop, make deals, and help tourists who were being overcharged. I helped them by negotiating with vendors to bring costs down. I loved doing this. It would make the vendor mad when I told them I was military, not a tourist. Italians love to use their hands when they talk to you. It was comical to watch them throw their hands around while yelling at me.

Going out to eat was a feast. Sometimes it took three hours. In Italy, they don't bring out your food all at once; rather, they serve by category—salad, vegetable, bread, meat, etc. A bunch of us and our wives found a seafood restaurant we enjoyed. The Italians rarely, if ever, baked or fried seafood. They boiled it. The server brought out a platter of octopus, squid, and other seafood. I loved the octopus. We were having such a great time, so why couldn't I let go of this habit?

Then the biggest mistake of my marriage happened while stationed in Italy. I convinced my wife's best friend to sleep with me. Afterward she felt so convicted that she told her husband and the chaplain in the chapel. I knew I was about to be exposed. I sat Sue down and told her. I felt so bad, because she never expected to be caught in the middle. I hated what I had done. I felt so ugly and dirty.

My chaplain called me into his office and talked to me about what I had done. There I sat, in a foreign country, with a chaplain I had barely had time to get to know. What I had not been willing to admit to anyone before him, I now confessed. I told him about my problem that I had been hiding for all those previous years. He told me, "You need to go to a mirror, look inside, stare at yourself, and say, 'Bob, I forgive you for what you have done.' Unless you forgive yourself, you will never get over this. If you believe Christ forgave you, then you need to do this for yourself and your family."

I thought about what he had said. I had to go home to face my family, but I couldn't go home right away. I hated myself. I didn't care anymore. *What's the use? I will never get over this. I might as well be what I am.* So, before I went home, I went downtown to the same ol' spot where the girls stood. I saw other soldiers trying to hook up, so I waited until they were gone. I didn't care anymore, so I hooked up. Afterward, I didn't want to go home.

I didn't want to face Sue. She had always been committed to me. I saw this big tree in the middle of a turnabout and pressed harder on the gas pedal. I was determined to smash my car into that tree when I heard this voice say, "Bob, what are you doing? Why are you trying to end your life? Are you ready to face God after what you did?"

You want to talk about coming to a sudden stop! I took my time driving home, thinking about what I had done. Remorse overwhelmed me. I wanted to blame someone, anyone, so I wouldn't hate myself so much.

## Vicenza, Italy

*It's not me that puts these thoughts in my head, God. Why won't you take them away? Look what you allowed to happen! Why do you keep ignoring me? I keep feeling like you set me up to fall. I'm trying so hard to learn about you, but I have this addiction that won't go away, and you won't take it away. Why not?*

I was extremely angry with God. I felt like I was being tossed between God and the devil, which I was, but by my own choice. I was the rag, and at every toss I was wearing thin. I needed to stop but still hungered for the immoral behavior.

When I walked in the door, Sue was sitting at the table waiting for me. I could tell she had been sobbing. "You need some help. Go see the chaplain tomorrow and get some help. I'm upset. I'm going to bed."

It took her months to forgive me. I ruined another couple's marriage, and our friendship with them. They left the army and moved on. We never heard from them again. Sue was very strong with her Christian faith, so I stood on that belief and hoped she would forgive me.

For the rest of my time in Italy, I kept away from the streets but kept looking at my magazines. I never wanted to give them up. I knew they were feeding my mind, but I felt like I had to have them. I felt a part of what I was reading. It made me feel like I was part of their magazine family.

One night as Sue was giving our daughter a bath, the chandeliers began waving back and forth. The previous week we had gone to the movie theater to watch the movie *Earthquake*. We knew then that we were having an earthquake. I picked up our little girl in a towel with her still gripping the soap.

The landlady took all the kids and put them in a van to protect them. We trusted the Italian people. Our neighbors loved the American children. A week later we took the kids and went to see the destruction that killed one thousand people. I will never forget the fear on my children's faces and the people running for safety. With only a crack in the hallway, our apartment weathered the earthquake with little damage.

One Sunday, we went to check out this Baptist church in Aviano, Italy, that our friends had told us about. The pastor was an American civilian who opened a church for the military to attend off base. Sue and I loved it, and so did the kids.

It was nice to get away from the military for one day. I had a great opportunity to talk with our pastor about my problem. I knew this made Sue happy, but, most of all, I needed to know why I wanted to continue looking at these magazines and why I always objectified women. I knew in my heart it was wrong, but I still wanted to look at them.

He read Romans 8:15–16. The apostle Paul also was struggling with old sin. Every time he tried to do right, he seemed to end up doing something wrong. Paul confessed in the Bible that he also was in a predicament. It felt great to me knowing that Paul, the one who persecuted the Jews, who turned to be a Christ follower and soul winner, knew the answer. In the last verse of Romans, Paul states: "Thank God through Jesus Christ. He has set us free."

Though I was wrestling with this sin of pornography, I knew I was forgiven by Christ. You would have thought that I might have gotten the point of forgiveness, but of course not. It seemed like every time I was getting closer to the Lord, here came that voice in my head, and of course I knew where

## Vicenza, Italy

it came from. That voice said: "Great news, Bob. You don't have to stop reading the magazines. Read that verse again. Even though you read those magazines, you will still go to heaven. It's an old habit that you just can't kick. You are the child of God. He won't kick you out of heaven. So, just keep them a secret and look at them. Who are you hurting? No one!"

The devil never told me how bad those thoughts would take control of my life, as he never does. I wanted to have a loving family, but this guilt of being with Sue's best friend kept bothering me. Learning about swinging and wife-swapping began to interest me.

*Maybe if I could get Sue to swap partners, it would be fun. I better not right now, but I will hint around and see how she would feel about it. I won't push her. But it might be fun.* Going back and remembering my thoughts back then still brings up many painful memories, but I do know who held my life in his hands all those years: It was Christ.

As I said before, Italy was my favorite assignment while serving in the military. The people were nice, and the young people loved American music and disco dancing. The Italian youth would always invite the Americans to a disco dance on the weekends, which many single soldiers went to, to have fun.

One day, my chaplain told me that he was tired of going to the sites by car, so he was going to request that we be flown out by a chopper on the weekends. The request was approved by our commander. I had never flown in one before, so I was excited but scared. When I compared a chopper to an aircraft, the chopper would come straight down, but the airplanes could glide down. *Oh well. What difference would it make? They both have to come down somehow*, I thought.

On Sunday morning Sue drove me to the landing pad. We stood there with my chaplain and our two children. Off in a distance we heard the noise of the chopper. As it came in for a landing, the kids' eyes got bigger. My chaplain and I walked over and got in, waving at Sue and the kids as we took off.

I noticed that Captain Smith was flying our chopper. He attended the local church where we did. I tapped him on the back and said hi. He pointed to a helmet to put on so I could talk to him. He asked the chaplain, "Where to first?" When we got to cruising altitude, the captain opened his window.

"Was he supposed to do that? Won't we blow up. Aren't we pressurized?"

I tapped the door gunner and pointed toward the captain's window. I nodded about it being opened. So, what does he do? He opens the door and looks out! I almost died looking down below us. My heart beat faster than the blades were spinning. Everybody in the chopper started laughing.

I didn't exactly appreciate their humor. After we landed, Captain Smith told me that choppers don't fly higher than 10,000 feet. I felt stupid after he told me that. I got used to flying in choppers, and on my last ride before I would be transferred to another unit in the States, Captain Smith had a surprise for me. He flew over the trenches that were dug out during WWII, and then we flew low over Jesolo Beach where people on the beach waved at us. Many times, we would fly over the tops of the mountains where people lived. They were used to the sound and smiled and waved to us as we flew by. I always had great chaplains who kept the faith.

They also put their trust in me to get the job done. I was a

## Vicenza, Italy

good worker, but I also liked to mix it up with them sometimes. One day I wanted to play a joke on the Catholic chaplain. During mass, the chaplain had to drink what was left of the wine in the chalice, so he always told me to pour only a little bit.

I knew how to set up mass, so on this day, I filled the chalice full of wine. The other assistant knew what I did and wanted to see the chaplain's reaction when he took off the cover.

When it came time to present the wine and wafers to the people, the chaplain uncovered the chalice and then looked to his side where we were laughing. It was his last mass before his transfer. At the time, he was not amused, but after the service he gave me a bottle of wine and told me to drink it. I told him, "I don't drink."

"The wine they give us here is awful, and you had me drink it all." Afterward the people kidded me about the full chalice. I told them it was just a joke. He grinned and said, "Don't turn Catholic."

During the weekends there was always something to do. If we weren't playing football or celebrating a holiday, we found some way to pass the time and enjoy our time in Italy. Each battalion had its own football team with rules like college. SETAF against the 71$^{st}$ airborne was always a classic, even a rivalry.

On July 4$^{th}$, the Italians would come on base and celebrate with us and watch fireworks at the end of the day. The last year and a half in Italy were an upper for me. I kept faithful to Sue and did not indulge with magazines. I will always remember the good times I had in Italy.

## Ten

# Fort Carson, Colorado

My next assignment was at Fort Carson, Colorado. As we were approaching the landing, the mountains peeked through the clouds, their majesty taking my breath away. We applied for housing on base and lived in temporary housing for a month while we waited for a duplex on base.

I thought, *I will keep faithful to Sue and the kids. I will find a church we can go to and be involved in. I will keep my bad habit overseas. I'm starting new here.*

My chaplain was primarily for soldiers who lived on post, while the main chapel was for soldiers and their spouses who had homes outside of base. For the most part, I could come and go as I pleased if I completed my work—typing sermons, bulletins, letters, and other clerical work. Therefore, I had plenty of time to spend with my family. Then came the news. Sue was pregnant with a little girl. I was thrilled to have another girl. I sometimes remind my daughter that she was born in an old medical building that was used during WWII, which since has been torn down.

The bubbly girl born there would eventually suffer because of her daddy in her young life. After my second girl's birth, Sue and I decided that three was enough, so that was it—two girls and one boy.

Life back in the States started out fine, but soon I went

back to my addiction. I always knew I had the chance to say no when I was tempted. I always had the tools to avoid falling into Satan's traps. Satan always attacked me in the same area—normal male feelings. I had never been taught how to control these feelings while growing up. I was instead taught how to complete these feelings until I got them again. Though my behavior was considered by many to be normal, I didn't know how to control it. I have always been told that it's my fault. So, I accepted it as my fault.

When it's always your fault, you sometimes crawl into your little shell. No one else matters. You will do whatever you need to make yourself feel good. Sad, but it's true. You can blame others, but it was always my decision. I felt bad about hurting people, especially the ones I loved, yet I would say to myself, *I am useless. I am no good to my wife or my kids. She is better off with someone else. I don't deserve her or anyone else. I feel like I don't want to be around her anymore.*

In church, people thought we were a great family. I sang in the choir with my wife and sang in the Christmas tree production during the season. I was able to give my testimony. I genuinely wanted to be a strong Christian. I might have put up a front, but I wanted to know more about being a Christian.

I had learned a lot being stationed overseas, yet I kept having irresistible sexual feelings. Time after time, I talked to people about Christ. I was a counselor at the youth camp but did not let go of my addiction. Erotic thoughts pounded in my mind. Day after day, my thoughts were fighting against each other. The only way to get rid of the pounding was to give in. I accepted the belief that when you're sexually tempted, it's better to just give in. Once I gave in, I thought the feelings would go away.

Since I couldn't, or wouldn't, let go of my habit, I gave up even trying to get rid of the habit. Downtown were prostitutes and adult bookstores.

Some weekends, I would drive around the block for hours, convincing myself to pick up a prostitute. I usually gave in. After awhile I went down there every weekend. I still hid the magazines and put on a front when I came home. I also continued putting up a front in church and doing my job at the chapel.

## Seeking Opportunity

Soon, I was promoted to Specialist 6, or SSG. I worked hard to get this rank and was proud to be an NCO. I loved when it was my time to pull duty NCO. One day, I came across the same premarital test that all chaplains gave to newlyweds they were counseling. I looked through it and came across a name. What did I do?

I planned the same course of action as I had at Fort Detrick, but this time it would do me in. I set up a day to meet with this woman who was in a bad marriage. I wanted her to take this test to see how compatible she and her husband were. As I sat on her sofa, I tried to convince her that her marriage was in decline.

She kind of stared at me with a strange look in her eyes until out of the bedroom came her husband. He yelled at me to get out. He would call my chaplain in the morning.

After the Vietnam War, military jobs were being replaced or dropped. Chaplains were getting out and returning to their homes to be pastors there, but what I had done was going to

## Fort Carson, Colorado

ruin my military career and my chance of retiring from the military at the age of forty-one.

My chaplain said that the post chaplain, a major, wanted to see me, so I reported to him. I knew I was going to be reprimanded but had no clue as to what was about to happen next.

"Specialist Gushwa, have a seat. I received a call from a very upset couple. Did you go over to their apartment to give them this test?"

"Yes, sir."

He continued, "I am very disappointment in you. Your record is clean, but now I can do only one of two things. I can throw the book at you and have you dishonestly discharged, or I can make a deal with you."

"OK?"

"I know in three months you can either reenlist or get out. I will turn my head on this issue and keep this between the two of us if you promise to ETS. What you did cannot be tolerated. It destroys our credibility, abuses the trust our office has developed with families, and we can't have this. Do you agree?"

"Yes."

I walked out of there relieved but angry because I wanted to stay in. I only had eight years to go. So now I had thrown away my retirement. A year prior to this, Sue and I had bought a house and fixed it up nice. Once again, I was planning to have a nice home with Sue and the kids, who were in school by then. At least Sue was working. She had a nice-paying job, so it wouldn't be so hard after I got out.

For the next three months, all I could do at work was hang around the office. They already had a replacement for me. I was planning for civilian life. I began seeking employment opportunities when I found an advertisement about being a truck driver.

There was a special offer for those getting out of the military, but the school was in Wisconsin. All I had to do was get there. It was a six-week course, and it seemed to be a good solution for our future. Also, I could go see my parents on the weekends.

I applied and was accepted for the school, but I still had three months before I got out. How would Sue take it? She would have three little ones to take care of while she worked an outside-the-home job. She would need to find a babysitter.

I was going through a rough time. My convictions about Sue, my habits, and my children were tearing me up inside. What I truly wanted, I didn't have. All the ingredients were there for a great marriage, yet I kept ruining our chances for a successful marriage.

Sue always was committed to our marriage, ever faithful, always loving and kind. I, however, was verbally abusive to her during our last year in the military. I let my frustrations out on her. She took it, but I couldn't continue being mean to her.

Like I said, you never get over the scars. This one I would remember and regret all my life. Nevertheless, I can't go back and reverse all that I did.

So here I was. I could have had a great life in the military, yet here I faced my last day there. I had an attitude about getting out, harboring anger toward the chaplain for putting me in this situation.

Yes, here I was, again, blaming someone else for my mistakes. I convinced Sue that we could still live in Colorado. I would get a job after school, although it was hard because the Vietnam War had ended and jobs were scarce. I always kept this bitter taste about not going to Vietnam. I hated the army for this. Now, it was time to get out.

Eleven

# Innocence Lost

No ceremonies. No celebration. Just handshakes and my Honorable Discharge Papers and DD214. I drove out of Fort Carson and have never been back since then. I picked up the kids from the babysitter and then went home. The moments of pleasure I took in the army with adult magazines and fulfilling sexual desires had prevented me from being able to reenlist.

When Sue came home, she knew I was upset, but she thought it was because I was being forced out and I would miss the military. She was right in part. I still do miss being in the military, but the choices I made left me in the end with no choice about the military. Sex and pornography are a powerful force. They wreak havoc on the home and on society. An addiction to them makes you regret to be alive, especially when you favor your habits over your marriage. Life after the military was about to take a big twist. For the next thirty years, I would take my habit to dark places.

## Deeper Still

I didn't go to truck driving school right away because I didn't want to leave the kids, so I delivered pizzas while Sue worked full time. I tried hard to stay in church, knowing it was important for me to somehow stay connected with some good in this world. I played racquetball with the pastor, taught Sunday school, and went to church youth camp, all the while struggling with impure thoughts of other women.

I tried my best to ignore the urges, to stay away from the porn, but I kept giving in. I became a bigger and better liar to keep up with my addictions. Money was tight, so I had to be more creative in fulfilling my desires. I loved my family, but I also loved my habit. Which would I choose? I couldn't keep both.

I knew I was a mess. I was willing to throw away my marriage because I was unwilling to change my behavior. Three young children who loved their daddy were about to lose him. That is hard to say, even now. When Sue came home one day, she brought a young friend who was going to babysit our children.

When I saw the babysitter, I never stopped to consider what the outcome would be if I pursued her. I never thought that my actions would break up my marriage. Maybe, deep down, I just didn't care anymore. I was convinced I was a man filled with his own lusts that couldn't or wouldn't ever change. A loving wife wasn't enough for me, so I got what I wanted in the downstairs basement. The babysitter and I promised to keep our behavior a secret, which she did. In May 1981, I finally went to truck driving school like I had planned after I received a grant from VA to take the class.

I told Sue, "I am going to school to learn how to drive trucks. Then I will try to get a job here local or run regional."

"What am I supposed to do about the kids? You won't be here to get them to school or see their school plays. Mike needs his dad. He's getting to that age."

"It will be only six weeks, then I'll be home."

She pressed, "When will I talk to you? We have no money for this."

"There are no good jobs here, Sue. I'm good at driving. That's what I like to do, so why not make money at it? I will get a job around here. I'll be back in six weeks."

She and the kids said goodbye to me at the bus station. I called them on the weekends, but I could tell this was not what Sue wanted for our marriage. She didn't want to raise the kids alone without a man, but I wanted to do this.

In Wisconsin, five of us stayed together in a house. *Oh great! Just what I need: more pornography.* All it took was picking up one magazine . . . again. It never failed. Pornography sought me out. I couldn't escape from it. Pornography became the normal way of life. If I didn't see the magazines, then I walked around feeling like something was missing.

I was beginning to feel this way toward women, also. *Once you cheat, what's one more woman anyway?* I was serious about driving and getting my CDL, so I made sure to do my best in classes. I took notes, but when it was my turn to drive, I was scared to death. I had to learn how to shift the transmission. I thought I knew all about driving a truck, but when it came time to be tested, I failed.

But there was a week extension class to go over where I failed. I stayed a week, and it was worth it. I passed. Before I went home, I visited my parents, where I also got my Class A license, there, in Indiana. I was proud of my first time getting a Class A license. *Maybe now I can put the military behind me.*

When I arrived home, my family was happy to see me. The babysitter never said anything to Sue, and she was there to smile at me when I returned home. She stayed the night, and the next morning I tried to pursue her again, but this time she rejected me.

"I can't do this to Sue. She is my best friend at work. If you don't stop, I'll tell her."

## Switching Gears

That was the last time I saw her because she told Sue that she was moving back to her mother's. Once again, I ruined someone's life. Did I feel bad? Yes, but only for a moment.

While Sue worked, I watched the kids and looked at the Help Wanted section for truck drivers. While doing this, I also read the house sitter ads. I continued looking until I noticed an owner/operator from Loveland, Colorado, who needed someone to drive one of his trucks. I was excited when I had a call back interested in me driving for him. Before taking the job, I would first go on a long run with him to make sure I could drive his truck.

Computers were starting to come out, but mostly in the business structure. I worked for an owner who leased out to a company called North American Van Lines. The owner delivered new computers to businesses. I did well with the owner, so he trusted me with his truck. I was gone on one run, then I was home for three days.

When I was home, I spent time with Sue and the kids. Our finances were doing better, and I loved driving a truck. Sue would run me back and forth between Loveland and our home. She met the owner and his wife, and I was beginning to believe we were turning a corner in our family.

Then, on one run, the tires were going flat and the truck

was breaking down. There was nothing I could do to control those circumstances. My employer let me go. Picking me up at the end of that ride, Sue asked, "Now what? What are you going to do now?"

"I'm going to drive somewhere else," I assured her, and within a week, I had a new job at Midwestern, located in Kansas. I had to run as a team. I was doing great with my habit, but when I was assigned to a certain driver, I didn't know he was into sleeping around. He was the main driver; I was the co-driver. He always knew where the ladies were, and he had their CB handles.

He gave me a handle that I always stuck with: "Fur trapper." It meant that I loved to chase after the ladies.

He also lived in Denver and would drop me off after we returned home. He once told me that I had a hot-looking wife. I knew it, but that was the first time any man had ever said that to me. When he said it, I remembered the articles I had read about wife swapping. Again, I let go of that thought, as I had enough trouble with porn.

Still, this guy loved to pick up the ladies. I sometimes went inside the truck stops and watched TV while he was "entertaining" the ladies. One night, he set me up with a "lady." It was my turn. I felt so dirty afterward. I couldn't stand myself. I wanted to get rid of the awful feeling but didn't know how. My heart felt so black and guilty.

So now, motivated by the images of my past burning in my mind, I was going to convince Sue to play into what I had already imagined. I would convince her. I called her long distance to ask her to just try it once. This was giving me a thrill. The lead driver asked Sue if she would like to go out on a two-week run with him. She said she had to think about it.

Encouraging her, I promised, "I will watch the kids. Go ahead and see what we do out there. You need to get away. You don't have to sleep with him if you don't want to."

"I will think about it."

I knew all along what was going to happen. When we got home, he convinced her to go with him. So, she took two weeks off work to go. When I watched her get in the truck and leave, I hated her. What I had just done was give my wife over to another man. Then, more than ever before, I hated my life.

I hurried and went to the newspaper to see if I could find another woman. I could not face the fact that I was a despicable man.

*She should have said no. Why did she leave so convincingly? I don't want to be married to her anymore. I can't face her every day. The only man she has ever been with was me. How could I be so evil. I am so guilty, God. What are you doing to me? How could you let this happen?*

*She shouldn't have gone! How can you let this happen, God? I was just curious to see if she would go.*

"Well guess what, Bob," answered God. "You got just what you wanted. There goes your wife into the arms of another man. That lovely Sue, the one who kept you to herself, and now you changed her. It's your fault. You were supposed to be the head of this family."

God was right, and I felt so angry that my stomach became sick. My heart sank, but it was too late because she had left. How was I ever going to face her? That day was one I will never forget. Everything I did in the past couldn't match what I had done that day with my sweet Sue, to my dear children, to our family.

The kids were in school when she left, so I had to make up an excuse when I picked them up. When I got home with my children, I sat them down and told them that Mom was getting away for two weeks.

## Help Wanted

While she was gone, I went back to the newspaper and found an ad in the babysitting section, which I called. A woman named Pam answered.

"Hi, my name is Bob. I'm answering your ad about babysitting. Have you ever considered house sitting?"

"I never have, but I would consider it because my son and I are living with my dad. I would love to get away from him."

"Why?"

"Because he is a drunk. When he gets mad, he starts yelling at me and my son."

"Yea. I need to get away too. My wife just left with another man on a two-week trip in his truck."

"Do you have any kids?"

"I have three."

"You don't really need a house sitter, do you?" *Wow, she gets me. I think she likes me.*

"You want to talk about this over dinner?" I asked.

"Sure."

I was determined to keep my children with me. I had to figure this out. Here I was willing to throw away my house and split up my family. I didn't have my magazines anymore because I didn't want Mike to get ahold of them, but what I was about to do to my marriage was a temptation from the devil but ultimately, my choice.

Satan is a liar. He destroys, deceives, and sets us up to

fail. As I look back now, I can see how God granted me so many opportunities to keep my family together. I thought about myself, not about my wife and children. I was willing to accept the consequences because I had no hope for myself.

The sins I had committed and would continue to commit ripped me apart from the inside out. Sending her on that trip with that man proved how far I was willing to go to take down my wife with me. I wanted her to feel bad too, but it backfired because of what I was about to do.

My first night with Sue away, I got a babysitter and had dinner with Pam. We hit it off right away. I came to dinner with a plan to convince Pam to go to South Bend, Indiana, with me and the kids. I was so sneaky that I planned this while Sue was gone. Sue always called at nights to talk to the kids, and I made it seem like everything was great at home.

I asked her how her "trip" was going. She admitted it was strange without saying much more about it at all. Still, she said she couldn't wait to come home. Little did she know that the house would be almost empty when she got there. My plan was to have her walk into an empty home unexpectedly, but I decided to stay put until I could find another house to rent.

*I think I'll ask Pam if she wants to move to South Bend with me and the kids. We can all live together. I need someone to watch the kids while I work, and she needs a home for her son too.*

The devil never let up. He knew how weak I was and would continue to put temptation right in front of me if I continued keeping my habits a secret. This is what happens when you remove your hands from Christ. You wander on your own.

Somehow, strangely enough, I believed I was enjoying this confusing lifestyle. This is what I wanted, what I read about, and my desire to experience it was greater than ever.

"Be careful what you wish for because you just might get it," as the old saying goes. In my case, getting what I wanted meant hurting others, even innocent others, like Sue and my children. The real problem I had with Sue was not her; it was me. I loved her so much that I hated myself. I had this burden that was hurting both my mind and my body. Every time when thinking about her with another man, my insides filled up with convictions that made me sick to my stomach.

I was the reason she had left. I knew that I was wrong, but I couldn't face her to admit it. I was a coward who ran away with my children. I always played smooth with people, and likewise with God, I tried to continue playing my ugly game.

*You saved me, and you can't go back on your word. I asked you to take this away. Apparently, you won't. I believe in salvation. I believe you died on the cross, rose again. I know that I am a sinner, and I have confessed my sins to you. I know that I'm forgiven, so I'll just continue to play around and go to church.*

Do you know how dangerous it is to say that to a sovereign God? I was mad at him. I was mad at me and mad at Sue, mad at the world.

## Separate Ways

Pam thought it would be great to get out of Colorado. We moved to South Bend, Indiana, and I would start my life over. Sue could have the kids over the summer, but I would raise them. My kids were my life, so why was I willing to drag them into another marriage?

I couldn't leave Sue hanging, so when she called, I told her I was leaving her and taking the kids to South Bend. There was silence on the phone, then crying. When I told her to stop crying, she reminded me that her going on the trip was my fault. She pleaded, "Wait till I come home, then we can talk about it. Don't leave me hanging. Why are you doing this, Bob? This is what you wanted, so you mean to tell me you tricked me into going so you could do this?"

Of course, I put most of the blame on Sue, but none of my accusations were fair. I was trying to erase my guilt. I decided to wait until she got home, but I wouldn't change my mind. When we did talk, it was always when the kids were gone.

Sue decided to stay with a friend of hers from church, and I would stay at the house until I moved. One day my car broke down at her job. She called a friend she met from one of her workers. It happened to be a guy, who gave me a jump, but before he left, I asked, "Are you dating Sue?"

"Yeah, kind of." Brad shrugged.

"We're separated, so I don't care. You can have her. We are through. You seem like a nice guy. You ought to marry her."

"Never thought about it, but nice to know that I don't have to worry about an ex-husband."

I asked Pam to move in with me, so she and her son moved in. I also managed to get a job, so the kids went back and forth to see their mother. I never took the kids out of their school, but instead I rented a house close to their schools. Every time I saw Sue, I burned with jealousy, but I was too proud to admit it.

I was willing to go forward, messing up my life instead of

admitting I was wrong. I never loved Pam. I was using her. She was my babysitter for the kids, but I kept my thoughts to myself. I played the nice dad act and still took the kids to church. The church knew we were separated, but I didn't care if they knew.

I didn't expect my children to like Pam, but they soon enjoyed her being around. I never talked badly about their mother to them either. Most of the time, I simply told them that we didn't talk about it. Life went on. Sue went her way, and me, my own pathetic way. I hated to see her because I still loved her.

I knew I had to figure out how I would raise my children. Also, I knew that I didn't want them to grow up like me, nor did I want Sue to have them. I was greedy, not willing to give Sue the comfort she deserved. She slept on a mattress at her friend's house, while the kids and I lived in our home.

Mike and my daughter were still in elementary school, so I thought I had a handle on them asking questions. They soon found out that their mom was sleeping on the floor and complained it wasn't fair for her to live like that. What was I supposed to do? I had enough trouble providing for the kids. I was working two jobs trying to support them even though Sue gave me money for child support.

Still, I never did forget about the magazines I had hidden. The memories of what I had read in the past were still current in my mind. I was determined to control Pam. Nobody was going to tell me what to do. Inside, my anger kindled, especially when I saw Sue with Brad. Not only was I angry, but also I was full of resentment.

I resented people who were close to God. I felt like I was one of his bad sheep, a nuisance to him. I had so little trust that I believed not even God could help me get out of this mess. I thought I knew better than him. After all, I would think, *What did he do when I cried out to him, Nothing! I just kept messing around. When I tried to get closer, he put his hand out as if he were disgusted with me.*

Those where my thoughts, yet somewhere in a quiet place of my soul, I knew God would never change to fit my habit. I could blame him for most of my problems, pointing my finger at him in anger, but God knew where I was, and he loved me through it all.

A sweet, loving marriage was crashing and burning, and I blamed God, but I knew it truly was my own fault. I had a choice to make: keep my magazines or keep my wife. I couldn't have them both without severe consequences.

The LIE: Time and again I lied to my wife, thinking she was dumb enough to believe me. Believing in myself was arrogance, but Sue was in love with me. She tried to figure out how our marriage had gotten so broken. She trusted me to tell the truth. For me, I was lied to by what I was reading in the adult books and magazines.

"All will be OK," said the devil. "It's human nature to have a sex drive, and if you can't control it, then you will have no choice but to seek others. That's just human nature. God created humans with the sex drive."

The BLAME: No matter how hard I tried to push the blame on others, the finger always pointed back at me. I was to blame. I knew what the Bible said about marriage. I went to marriage retreats. I sat in the pew, listening to many sermons about having a happy marriage.

The CHOICES: I don't care how old you are, if you can make choices, then you are accountable for them. I never loved Pam, but she did love me. So now I found myself having to put up another front. This would be more difficult to accomplish than in times past.

*How can I do this? How can I stare in her eyes convincing her that I love her when I know I don't?*

I filed for divorce like a coward would. Sue and I agreed not to drag the kids into this, but that was unavoidable. We agreed that I would have custody of the kids, but Sue would have them in the summer. This was settled out of court to keep the cost down. Could I ever put this behind me?

Fearing to be alone more than anything, I asked Pam to marry me. She said yes. My heart said no, but I put up a front. We decided to get married at the Veterans Memorial in Memorial Park.

My children came to the quiet wedding ceremony. There was not a reception, just a dinner with Pam and the kids. Here I was married again. Nothing ever changes when you live in sin. God was patient with me, to a certain point.

After I said my vows, I checked to see if I had crossed my fingers or toes. The marriage was final, but I knew from the start I would not be totally committed. I was bitter, because here I was slapping Sue in the face by getting remarried right away. It seemed like her life was better than mine, and I knew it would be difficult to raise the kids. *But whose fault was that?*

## The Babysitter's Marriage

I was too selfish and stubborn to make my first marriage work, so what would ever make me think that my second marriage would be any different? I thought because I had my children at the time, there might have been a chance I could do better. However, the truth was I had become so bitter, my second marriage was doomed to fail also.

While my children were the only bright spot in my life and they always made me feel good, feeling good wasn't what I needed. Acting as if I had all the answers, I always had to have the last word. I was the man full of opinions, and anyone who crossed me discovered I was always right. I couldn't hold a dialogue, because I wouldn't let others speak what was on their minds. Truth be told, I was afraid they might be right, which in mind would have meant I was a failure and a fake.

Every time I turned around, I was wrong. I was getting on my own nerves because I had to figure out how to turn this situation around to make me feel and sound good, especially when the kids were listening. I didn't want them to see how torn up their dad really was inside.

I felt like I was in the middle of a fight between God and the devil, and that wasn't fair. It was God's fault for allowing the devil to mess with my family. It's not that I hated God, but I was terribly upset with him. I thought I knew better than God what was best for me and my life. So, I thought!

I had to get away from Sue. I was afraid she might get an attorney and fight for custody of the kids, so I sold my little girl's cute dogs, loaded the U-Haul, and moved to South Bend with all the kids and a pregnant cat. When we arrived at my parents' house, my dad refused to let the cat into the house, and it was wintertime! Fueled with another fresh reason to hate my dad, I stayed in the car with the cat.

Pouting was my expertise, even though it never got me anywhere. The next day, we gave the cat away.

Nothing ever changed with my dad, although I didn't

help matters much. With the mistakes I kept making, my dad had reasons to criticize me. No matter what I said, nothing positive came out. Ultimately, I had to figure out this life on my own. While I could have turned to God for help and restoration, I kept him out of my decisions. I had messed up, so why should I expect God to fix my life?

I had to find a place to live and a job, not to mention I had to feed my family and money was running out. In fact, the money had run out, and we needed financial assistance from the government. In order to get that help, I had to do community work first. Nothing was just handed out back then, which was the way I preferred it.

After applying for welfare and food stamps, my self-image declined even more. I had always been able to work and make money, even from an early age. Depending on the government to support my family was humiliating. I knew that I could get a job as a driver somewhere, but where?

When I was volunteering for community work, I visited the work force center to find a job. I found an ad for a driver at a van custom shop to deliver converted vans to dealers throughout the country. Just my field. I applied and got the job. I was concerned about leaving my kids with Pam, but figured I had to take the job.

## On the Road Again

We moved in, and I started working. Things seemed to be going great, even though I had returned to my former habits. Buying magazines was more important than seeing to it that my family's needs were met. I lied on my monthly income statement required by the food stamp office and got caught doing so.

For the first time in my life, I was forced to appear in

court. I was charged with a misdemeanor and sentenced to one hundred hours of community service. I decided to tutor a foreign student to speak English, which only lasted a month because I quit when she refused to date me.

While driving the vans across the country, I managed to meet other women. Since I didn't love Pam, I figured this gave me an excuse to cheat on her. *Why not? I cheated on Sue, so why not Pam too?*

The downhill fall continued. The Lord allowed me to continue making my own decisions. I didn't know what God was doing, and if I had, I wouldn't be where I am at now. God always had watch over me.

Pam, the kids, and I kept moving from house to house when the rent came due because I wouldn't have enough money to pay rent. More accurately, rather, I had enough money coming in from my job, but I would spend a lot of it on topless bars and pornography.

I never liked to leave my kids when I worked, but I had to keep making money. Pam and I decided to go to a different church that was closer to our home. It was an enjoyable place to gather on Sundays, but the pastor made the real difference with me. In time, the pastor would reveal something that would shock me.

After being on my job for about six months, I noticed that some of my money was missing from my wallet. My job depended upon me cashing the checks my employer gave me. I was to cash the check, take the van to the dealer, then find my way back. Without all the money, I couldn't do my job.

Every time I found the money, it was always in my daughter's belongings. I couldn't figure it out. Pam tried to convince me that my oldest daughter was stealing from me, but she was too young to understand money. One day, I brought everybody into the living room.

"I don't know who is taking my money, but I need the money back to deliver this van. Whoever is taking it is preventing me from doing my job. Whoever is taking my money, put it back."

Nobody put it back, so I had to end up borrowing money. Then it happened again. This time *all* of it came up missing. I found some of the money in between the mattresses of my daughter's bed, so I took her to her room to spank her. I kept telling her that I needed the money, and she kept telling me she didn't have it.

After I saw I was putting marks on her, I rushed out the door crying. *What had I just done?*

I managed to get the van delivered, not knowing what was about to happen when I got back. The guilt of what I had done disturbed me so much that I had to talk to someone, so I went down to the church to speak with our pastor, who then opened my eyes to what had been happening in my own home.

He started, "I think I know who has been taking your money."

"Who?"

"Your wife."

"You mean to tell me that I took it out on my daughter, and my wife stood there watching me?"

"I'm so sorry, Bob. I believe something happened in her past, and she was saving up in case it was to happen again. She is insecure and is saving up money in case you run with your kids."

"Oh, I'm so angry! How could she just sit there knowing

that she stole from me and letting my daughter take the punishment for something she didn't do. Nobody does this to my children. That's it!"

Instead of listening to my pastor, I stormed out of the church, loose as a cannon, ready to take out the full vengeance of my life on Pam. Fearing I would do something crazy, I sat in my car to calm down first. After admitting to myself that *I* was the one who had created this mess, placing myself and my kids in this predicament, I knew I couldn't bear to make them suffer with me any longer.

I wasn't sure how I ever was going to get out of this one. The best way out was to give my children to their mother. This was just another sharp arrow in my heart. I had boasted in my heart that I had taken the kids from their mother. Now it was backfiring on me.

## Losing Children

I called Sue to tell her what had happened. Even though she had married Brad, I knew my kids would be in good hands with her. Sue explained she would have to discuss the change with Brad first. They already had his two boys living with them. Their small house would then have to accommodate two adults and five children.

I knew that the children would be going back to the church they once attended. I knew they would grow up better in the Christian faith, better than the way I was raising them. They had witnessed too much of my weaknesses, my failings, and not enough peace.

I decided to fly the kids back to their mother before making plans to deal with Pam. I never did tell Pam that I knew about what she did until the kids were gone. When I saw the kids leave, I was hurting but relieved that they would grow up in a stable home with their mother. Sue told me not to send child support because I had bigger issues to deal with.

I did send what I could at Christmas time. Sue never put me down in front of the children. She always told them, "He is your father. You still respect him. I will not talk about him behind his back to you kids. You can still talk to him on the phone and see him if he comes here to visit."

After the kids moved out from my home, I went back on the road, staying there as often as I could to avoid Pam. One weekend I figured out how I would get my money back from her. With her son in the back seat, I got my money back in a weekend. Was I proud of what I did? Absolutely not.

I once again moved to another house with Pam and her son. After I got my money back, I dropped the subject, but it really wasn't over in my head. Here I was with a second wife, and I still couldn't make it work. I was bitter at my past and everyone that was in it. Here I was amounting to nothing while Sue had a great job, and Brad was working also.

*Am I that stupid that I just can't see?* I sobbed. *I know what I have been doing is wrong, but I can't help myself. I only know one way to deal with these sexual feelings. I don't know any other way, so how am I supposed to go on?*

The voice spoke up, "Did you enjoy the magazines, the bars, the women? C'mon! Do you really want to give that all up? It's too late to turn around. You've been enjoying it too long. You can't go back, so just enjoy more of it."

While I was driving on my job, Satan was able to distract me from the reality of who I was. On the road, I was reliable, a safe driver, a friendly guy. On the road, I was also an empty bucket where Satan could pour into me his vile thoughts.

## Innocence Lost

Nobody was around to keep me distracted from him. That's when he always attacked my thoughts.

I always concentrated on the feeling of what he was saying rather than on the truth I knew deep in my heart. Life was not precious to me like it should have been. When I look back now and see all the lives I hurt, many of all ages, I am more convinced that God's mercy and grace truly will follow me all the days of my life (Psalm 23:6).

After we moved again, I befriended a nineteen-year-old girl named Monica who lived across the street, although my motives were beyond "just friends." I convinced her to follow me in a rented car to a dealer where I was delivering a van. I told her that I would pay her to come with me.

She was excited about getting away from her old boyfriend and town. After delivering the van, we started back home, but I suggested we stop at a motel, to which she agreed. After we got back, for about four months I continued to see her whenever Pam was gone.

Now that the kids were with their mother, I felt like I had no use for Pam anymore, so I moved to a nice apartment complex. One night I picked up Monica to go out when she told me she was pregnant.

Although I knew it wasn't mine, I pretended that it was. I knew very well that it was her ex-boyfriend's baby because I couldn't have any more children. She told me how she wanted to get an abortion. I was so lost in my mind for sexual habits that I went along with her.

## Ending a Life

Monica was determined to get an abortion even though she had no money. Her ex-boyfriend came to my car door window and tried to break it, and then we argued. I told him, "Yeah, I know it's your kid." The ex-boyfriend wanted her to have the baby and let him raise the child. She refused to be persuaded, so she came to me for the $150 she needed for the abortion. I was trying to get out from underneath this "pregnant thing" and felt like I needed to help her too. Truthfully, it was between her and her boyfriend, which is where it should have stayed.

I didn't like seeing her in pain, so I gave her the money. She called and found out that she had to cross over the state line into Michigan to have the abortion. It would be an outpatient procedure, so I waited for her outside in the old truck. All I could think about was this doctor tearing apart this little baby. *This is my fault.*

Holy Spirit: "You're sitting in your truck while this little innocent baby is being tortured with knives. This baby is being abused by its doctor, and you're partly at fault. You paid that doctor to do it. You had no right to end a life.

"Being a child of God, knowing that this is wrong will bring much burden on you until you realize what you have done and come to Christ with this. Until then, your life will continue going down the path of destruction, one thing after another. But remember, I still love you, Bob."

Weeping in my truck, I was frozen with a flood of emotions. I couldn't stop the abortion. Legal abortion was new at the time, and many women ended up hemorrhaging sometimes after the procedure. Some women went through difficult reactions after giving up their child. So here I had one more miserable, self-inflicted scar I would have to carry all my life.

After the surgery, Monica came walking back to the

truck. When she sat down, I could see she was shivering, so I brought her over to my place. Walking up the stairs caused her to lose a lot of blood, so I called the ambulance. She ended up staying in the hospital for three days to recover.

I decided that I couldn't live like this, so I went to her place to encourage her to get back with her boyfriend. However, before I could get out of my car, her boyfriend stood at my car window ready to kill me. Knocking on my window, he yelled, "You killed my baby, and now I'm going to kill you! Get out of the car. You're a dead man."

"I'm not getting out. Go back to your girlfriend. Blame it on her. She is the one that chose to get it done. I just gave her the money. Go away, you loser, or I might just come out and give you the chance."

I drove away before the situation got out of hand. The next day Pam moved back in with me.

Every day my life was being wasted away living in sexual sins. What confused me the most was why God wouldn't take these desires away. Why was he allowing this to happen? How could a born-again Christian do the things I was doing? Many times, Satan tried to convince me that I was lost, but I knew better.

I knew that my heart was tearing me up inside because my convictions were strong after every encounter, whether with magazines, adult stores, or women. What made me so mad was my vision of God allowing Satan to tempt me. I thought God was on my side. Sometimes I felt the Lord's presence, but most of the time I felt the attacks by the devil. One thing for sure, I was being educated about the world of immorality, but still I hated the results and the consequences.

*How could this be my fault?* I called upon God to help

me. Instead, I get the devil attacking me. Later, I learned I was in the middle of a fight. One voice called for obedience to God, while the other called for complete abandonment of morality, compassion, and reason. I was listening and doing the damage that Satan convinced me to do. *So, what happened, God?*

What I had learned and read in the Bible wasn't happening to me. So many Christians in our church were living a life close to God. I wanted to stop living wrong. I made so many attempts to quit, but I would start back up again. After awhile I just gave up, thinking, "What's the use?" I couldn't get rid of these thoughts.

Searching for another home for Pam, her son, and myself, all I could find was an old house that I convinced the landlord not to tear down. It was full of bugs, so I tried my best to spray it down to get rid of them.

Driving around town, I noticed a sign in a fast food restaurant window looking for a night manager. I was hired for the job and quickly began working my way up to a shift manager position. I enjoyed working the graveyard shift, but when my truck broke down, I had to walk and take the bus to work. I had a great crew who worked for me on the night shift. I told them that if we finished our work early, we could sit around waiting till the next shift. They were hard workers. Many daytime workers asked to work night shift because I was easy-going and fun to work with on our shift. I loved teasing this one girl named Denise, but there also was something about her I liked.

When we were alone, we would talk easily with each other. She told me how much she was struggling with going through her divorce. Instead of trying to help her save her marriage, I began blasting her husband as a bad man who didn't deserve to have her. This was my usual strategy. Once again, I was "the man with all the answers."

I asked her how she got home from work. She said sometimes she walked or took the bus. On this night, it had snowed hard, and the buses weren't running, so I walked her home. My relationship with her continued, taking her home occasionally in a taxi. Each time, I told her how much I cared for her, and then before I knew it, we were hooking up.

While Pam was home asleep with her son, I was messing around with another woman. Denise was seventeen years younger than me with two precious little girls, but that didn't matter to me. We continued to work together, and I continued to walk her home.

My brother had brought over an old truck with a hole in the floor for me to use. One night I took a bag with a deposit to the bank. When I got to the bank, the bag was missing. I looked for it, but it was nowhere to be found. I drove back and forth but found no bag. *Oh no! What am I going to tell the store manager? It must have fallen out down the hole. I thought I put it on the seat. It must have fallen on the floor. Now I will lose my job.*

I denied ever stealing the money, yet they made me take a polygraph test. I failed it, but I knew I was telling the truth. I never took the money. It had fallen on the pavement. Somebody got some money that day. Instead of firing me, they transferred me to another store. I kept the same truck and was a shift manager during the day.

Denise and I became serious, and I thought it best to tell Pam about what I was doing and what I planned to do. I intended to divorce her and move back to Colorado with

## It Only Takes One Look

Denise and the girls. I had no remorse for divorcing Pam. I always blamed her for me losing my kids. That's what I always did—blame someone else.

I stayed with Denise at her place. Pam applied for welfare and food stamps and moved in with a friend she had met. Like Sue, I was to blame for the infidelity in my marriage. I had only looked to satisfy my own sexual needs. So, here was number two going into my legacy. *What will my kids think of their dad now?*

I could come up with an excuse. Denise had two little girls, and I thought my kids would love them. However, by then my oldest daughter was a freshman in high school, and Mike was a senior. I needed to get back to Colorado, but how could I? I had no vehicle. Pam did her best to come between Denise and me. She only fueled my anger for her. One such incident I recall went something like this:

"Take your boy and leave me alone. I will file for divorce," I threatened.

"I don't want a divorce. Come back, Bob, please. Stop doing this."

"No. Get away from my truck before I call the cops. I never did love you, especially after what you did to my daughter. I hate you for this."

Trying to turn the tables, Pam yelled, "I will file for the divorce! You don't have to!"

I drove away, and that was the last time I ever saw her. I moved in with Denise and her two daughters, and I convinced the girls that I was going to be their stepdad. So ended marriage number two. No lessons learned. I would take all my destructive habits into the next chapter of my life.

## Twelve

# How Long, Lord?

I used the same truck (the one with a hole in the floorboard), and the same situation happened again. I was taking the deposit to the bank on the way home. When I got to the bank, I looked for the bag, but it was gone. *Oh no! What am I going to tell them? They will think I stole the money for sure, but I didn't. Now I'm going to be fired. No job! I could just leave Denise and the girls and go back to Colorado. Nah. I can't do that. I really like this woman.*

When I told my boss what happened, he called the police, and once again I had to take the polygraph. Once again, I failed. I never did take their money. Twice it fell through the hole in the floor. That truck jumped around so bad, no wonder the deposit bags fell out. I did my best to convince them that I would never take their money, but they still fired me.

*Now what am I going to do? Everything I try, I mess up. I can't stay married. I love my porn magazines. I love looking at women, wishing I could have them. I wish I was dead. I wish I had taken my gun and killed myself. I hate hurting these innocent women. What am I saying? Am I now getting a soft heart for people?*

I wanted to move back to Colorado to be close to my children. They were getting older, and I didn't want to miss out on their lives. My sister gave me a car her late husband had left her. I was to give her money when I got back on my feet. I packed the car and a U-Haul with Denise and the girls and moved back to Colorado, where I found an apartment right next to where Sue and the kids lived.

Once there, I unloaded with the help of my kids. What made the apartment so great was it had a pool, so my kids often came over. I went back to the church where Sue and I used to attend. It was strange at first because Sue and my children were attending also.

Denise and I talked with the assistant pastor about getting married. He counseled us, especially about the age difference. We decided to have a short ceremony with my children present.

*This marriage is going to work, even if it kills me*, I thought. I had everything I needed. I could see Sue, be with my children, attend my former church, and start over with a new marriage. I was determined to make it work. Sue and I got along well, and I got along well with her husband. I was happy Sue had a great husband who truly loved her. I still loved her, but I had to keep that a secret in my heart. My children got along with Denise and her two girls also. They all loved to go swimming in the pool.

## Another Marriage, Another Job

What I needed to do next was get a job. Knowing this was one thing I was great at, I went downtown and applied for an over-the-road truck driving job. Leaving Denise and her daughters behind might not be the right idea, but I decided to take a chance.

Once again, I loved truck driving. I traveled a lot and became familiar with this large trucking company. I had to start fresh, so for two weeks, I went out as the second driver. After this I was given one of the older trucks to ride solo. One good thing about the job was I could park my trailer in the company yard in Denver, then drive down to Colorado Springs for a week off. As a truck driver even in an older truck, I managed to be good at shifting and driving up and down the mountains, plus I kept a clean and safe driving record.

One day I was asked if I wanted to have a brand-new truck. The catch was, I would have to train the new drivers coming out of school about the operation of the company. I was finally going somewhere in my life. Accepting the promotion greatly increased my income, which was always a good thing at first. That is, it was good until I messed it up.

Of course, while being an OTR driver, I couldn't stay away from the ladies and the magazines. I would praise the Lord with one side of my mouth, then turn my attention toward addiction once again. I took being a good driver for granted. I thought I had it made, until I was hit hard by Satan.

It was a deliberate attack—one I never saw coming until it happened. I won't go deep into it, but if you follow along, you will guess. I loved being able to come home and see my family. I always had extra money to spend on the kids, went to the church with them, and continued my relationship with Denise.

In about two months, Denise and I sat down again with the associate pastor to be counseled about getting married. A month later, we got married in the smaller church with all the girls there. I taught junior high Sunday school class, until I made a mistake, which was kept quiet. I felt so wicked inside. I despised what I had become. I hated being myself.

I was so angry with God, once again, for allowing this to happen. I was so disrespectful to God at the time: *God, how could you let this happen! I hate what I did. I am nothing. I know I'm nothing to you. You call yourself so holy and righteous, but I did this. How can I be YOUR child? How can there be a heaven full of perfect people?*

*Where does that leave me, because I'll never be perfect. Because I'm talking this way to you, you will probably kill me. How could you let this happen? I feel like you betrayed me. I keep trying to get over this, but you let me keep going back. Why won't you take this away from me?*

*Whyyyyy?!!!! I'm scared to go to church now. Are you happy? Is this what you want? Then I won't go anymore. Do you have your favorites that you take care of? Well, I'm not one of them. Am I?*

How did I ever get turned around after talking like this to the Lord? I didn't for a while. It got worse, much worse, so much worse that I never expected to get through it. My heart grew more bitter. What I hated in life, I did. What I had read, I did. The apostle Paul could have related with me, although at the time, I didn't see the connection.

Paul cries out in Romans 7:15, "I do not understand what I do. For what I want to do I do not do, but what I hate I do." God gives us the freedom to choose right from wrong. I have always been without excuse because my conscience told me right from wrong, yet I continued to make the wrong, bad choices. I always chose to look back over my shoulder to my perverted past, and when I did that, I gave in.

My heart knew right from wrong, and talking to God as though I did not was totally disrespectful. My heart was searching for an easier way to obey him. I wanted to take the past and throw it away, but every time things were going great, Satan would come at me like a lion stalking its pray.

*Why me? Why do you think you have to pester me? I might be a pathetic person, but I have one thing you can never have—my soul. I know the truth about Christ. I know you're a loser. Satan, you are the deceiver and liar. Leave me alone. I don't want you to bother me. I'm going to start over and do things the right way. I want to make God happy, not you. GO AWAY!*

Ready to change, I went back to church, although there was one thing that kept bothering me. Every time I knew I had sinned and kept running back to my old ways, I would return to Christ and ask for forgiveness. I knew I was saved, but I wanted him to forgive me and help me get rid of the messed-up lifestyle I had adopted.

I felt like God wasn't listening to me, but I learned later that it was me not listening and obeying him. I was living a life of disobedience. Christianity was frustrating me. I never expected to have gone through what I did, but who does?

How many of us know about tomorrow? If I knew about tomorrow before I went to bed and it was bad, why would I want to wake up? Many times, I didn't want to wake up. Things seemed to have settled down after I returned to church. Only God and I knew the extent of what I had done.

My normal routine of going out on the road for three weeks and coming home for one week had returned. When I was home, I walked the girls to school. Denise also worked part time. Sounds stable, right? However, I continued the cheating and reading my adult books and magazines, which I refused to give up.

One afternoon I had a deliberate attack by the devil

catching me in a moment where I did not stop and think about consequences once again.

## A Thief Surrenders

Sometimes, temptation catches you off guard. It just happens. This was one of those times. The timing and setup were perfect for me to fall into Satan's tricks. But this time, I would take someone with me down that dark, ugly road that would last for almost five years. He taught me how to manipulate, threaten, hide my actions, lie, blackmail, blame others, and take no personal responsibility. Innocent people would be involved and hurt.

After just one time, I gave up. *I am what I am. I know now that I can't stop being like this. Since God won't stop Satan, I'll just go along with him. Nobody can say I didn't try.*

I kept up a front so as not to get caught. All I thought about was myself. Just like before, it was about me. I could tell people how to be saved, but then I lived my own life like the devil. I led an entire family to Christ, so how could I continue to live such a sinful life? I knew that people needed Christ to be saved and knew how to lead them to the cross. Yet, the same convictions were overwhelming me.

I was in a battle of my life. I knew that Satan was my enemy, yet I continued to listen to him. I took advantage of the love of Christ to continue what I was doing. *Jesus loves me no matter what I do wrong, including this.* I kept convincing myself that I would never get caught. I enjoyed what I was doing even though I knew it was wrong. I had someone to love me, but I knew once again that what I was doing was ungodly, disobedient, and destructive. Sooner or later, I would get caught.

A week later, my stomach began to turn every time I was around the family, as I would have to keep what I had done a secret. If somebody knew, I would be in deep trouble.

So why didn't I quit? It was stuck in my mind that I had to have images. I was scared of what I might be without them. They had become a part of me. It was who I thought I was. I knew all along they were bad for me, but as the years went by, I became addicted. The longer my mind entertained those impure thoughts, the more I wanted. I never knew how powerful lust was.

When you're so addicted, sooner or later you will believe your desires are a necessity. You will use whatever or whomever you can to get your satisfaction. I knew in my heart that God would not tolerate my actions much longer, and then I would be in deep trouble, but who could I turn to for help? In this instance, I knew there was nobody that could help. This was one mistake that had to be kept a secret from everyone.

I remember when one of Denise's daughters made an innocent comment to Denise. Denise asked me about it, but I blew it off. A mother, however, never lets go of a feeling sparked by a thought or a passing comment. For three years, Denise kept that comment hidden in her heart, but she still allowed me to be around the girls. I wanted help so bad. I wanted to stop all this. *If God won't help me, who will?*

I kept going back to my sexual "reader's guide," which taught me more about accepting my sinful habits as natural and healthy. I had tried everything else, so why not this? It was enticing, and hardly anybody else could say that they had tried it. It would make me special, more experienced than others.

The deeper I kept going into sexual sins, the more remorse I was beginning to have. The guilt was tearing me up. I knew what I had to do, but I was so embarrassed to go to God. I started believing the lie that was hovering over me, who I was created to be. *I didn't ask to be this way, so I must have been born this way.*

Instead of trying to get help, I was trapped into thinking I had to see and get more. The more I went after it, the more I opened myself to being caught. At the same time, another voice was telling me I would get caught. It was a warning to STOP and come forward, but I wouldn't listen. I knew who that voice was, where it was coming from, and how to ignore it.

*I just can't come before you, God. I have done a most wicked sin. You said that it would be better for me to drown then to ever harm one of these. So how can I come before you? I hate what I am doing. Nobody could ever understand what I have been going through. If you understood, then why did you let me do this? I hate me, I hate looking in the mirror. There is no hope for me now. Just do what you must do to me.*

*Now I am considered a sex offender. Now people will hate me. I will have to pay for all this stuff. I haven't been caught yet, but when I am, I will lose everything. Why can't I stop?*

I wanted to tell Denise what I had done, but I didn't realize that she was torn up inside but kept it to herself. I suggested that she get some help. She never knew that I had continued what I was doing.

*What am I doing, suggesting that she gets help? If she does get help, they will have to turn this into the cops.*

Eventually, Denise fell into a deep depression. I knew it was my fault. She trusted me with the girls, and all I did was drive a savage knife in her heart. I knew that I was hurting her inside, and I wanted her to get help, but I needed her to leave me out of it.

One afternoon before going out on another run, I took her to see a female psychologist while I waited in the car. I knew I was in trouble when she didn't come out for a long time. Then I noticed her walking out with her counselor. Denise waited in the distance while the counselor talked to me through my window.

"Bob, you need help. This can't go on any farther. I will give you twenty-four hours to give yourself up and get help, or I will report you. Do we agree?"

"Yes," I said, head hanging, "but where do I start?"

"I suggest you start at social services."

On the way home, I tried to turn myself in at social services, but they had never heard of anyone turning themselves in, so they directed me to the police department. I drove over and told Denise that if I didn't come back out, to just go home. An officer led me to an office where two detectives questioned me. This was the first time they had ever had someone turn himself in.

I was scared to death, but I did tell the truth. I wanted this out in the open, although I was in shock because I never expected to be sitting where I was. After I told them what I had done, they released me, instructing me to stay away from my family. The next morning, the detectives interviewed the girls to discover all our stories matched.

A court date was set up, so I figured I would be away from Denise and the girls. I was so arrogant, thinking that it wasn't a big deal that I decided to go back out on the road, but the detectives warned me it wouldn't be in my best interest to leave. I needed to deal with this "big deal" first. That same day, I drove up to the truck yard to take my things out of my truck. I told my trainee that he would be reassigned to another driver. I told my regional manager that I needed some time off. I made up a lame excuse, then I drove off.

My life was no longer in my hands. All of what I had read and did felt great for a quick moment, but it wasn't so great when the detectives took me down to booking. The judge allowed me public bail. I could not move back in, so I took all my 401K and stayed in a cheap motel.

When I moved out, one of the few things I took with me was my computer. While waiting for three months with nothing to do, I discovered many porn sites and chat rooms. Some of the chat rooms were for teens, so I thought it would be funny to play a role of an aroused teenage boy. I came up with a fake picture and then spent my days doing what I had always done, searching for more pleasure at any expense. I was sick mentally, but I was never willing to accept the full blame for my actions. I had no empathy for women or girls. I used my past as an excuse to sin.

## Welcome to the Web

Sitting in the motel, searching and talking on the computer, feeling bad at times only for getting caught, I continued to feed my sickness. I always blamed my condition on other people. I always knew I was wrong but was too proud to admit it. I knew I needed help, but most of the time, I didn't want help. I wanted more of what made me feel good.

One of the hardest things to explain is why I knew that what I was doing was wrong but kept doing it. Why was I so willing to continue going down the steep slope? After the first time, why didn't I stop? I can best explain it this way: I believed that what I wanted I needed, and what I needed, I had to have. As a believer in Christ, I should have known that sin always began as a thought in my mind. The thoughts always entertained and excited me the more I dwelled on them. The more I kept thinking about them, the more my body reacted to the thoughts. My mind and body were reacting together.

The devil knew my weakness. He tempts your eyes to wonder what's new in the magazines. Then your thoughts go beyond the pictures in the magazine to the real thing. Then your mind tells your body you need to do something about it or you're going to explode. Am I right so far?

To an extent, yes, my body would have never reacted to my mind if I weren't thinking impure thoughts. I wouldn't have had impure thoughts if I hadn't been filling my mind with lewd books and magazines.

In most cases, someone innocent will pay the price for your mistakes. In my case, many did. But God never let go of me. At the time my mind was so full of lust that I wouldn't listen to Gods warnings.

But one day soon, he was going to get my total attention. So, I sat in this motel, filling my mind up with what got me here. I had it in my mind that I would get what was coming to me. I hated my heart, because it kept my mind twisting. My conscience, my heart, and my mind were tearing up my body. I was trying to make sense of it all but never got serious about it.

*I am a loser. Who would ever do what I just did? I hate myself. I am now ruined for life. But I just must accept myself as a pervert. Not even God wants to help me. He had all those years, but did he ever take this away? NO! He kept ignoring me, letting me wander with no answers.*

*A sex offender. Is this what I am? Do you see me this way, God? I thought I was your child. How can this be? You would never let us in your heaven. Hold on a second, God. Did I not confess ALL my sins to you? Did you not forgive me? I sat pouting.*

## Broken Treatment, Recovery Denied

The judge sentenced me to four years of treatment. A committee would oversee my progress. I eventually moved up to the Denver area and got a job picking up trash. I finally had a full-time job, but I would have to make up an excuse to get off early every Tuesday. I lied to my employer, telling them I was going to school. Truth was I had to drive back and forth to Colorado Springs every Tuesday for class.

I knew better than to slip up because I would then have to go to jail. I also had to keep a job and pay for treatment and polygraphs. One thing I always had going for me was working. I always had to work. This class finally gave me a chance to sit and think about myself. But something was wrong. They weren't teaching how to stop, but instead they were teaching me how to manage my feelings and when to know how to manage them. All this did was put more pressure on controlling myself.

*Lord, what do you think about all this teaching? You kept telling me that I had to stop fornicating and committing adultery. They are telling me that I can still have sex with adults over twenty-one after I complete treatment. What am I to learn from all this? I feel like my head is going to explode. They say I must keep what YOU say to myself. So now what?*

I was shocked when the male counselor, pointing to the female therapist standing next to him, said to this one guy in front of us all, "You want to have sex with her, don't you?" I almost walked out. It was all I could do to sit there and listen to what they were saying. From that time on, I despised being in treatment. Most of the time, I just sat there thinking about where my life was heading.

The day came when some of us had to go in front of the committee to see how we were doing in treatment. Then, we found out the committee was going to break up and that we would be put on probation instead.

"That wasn't part of my sentencing. I'm not going to move back to Colorado Springs. I feel betrayed. I'm trying to get through this."

At the appointment with my probation officer, all I heard from her was threats and put-downs. When I left her office, I felt like I was the filth of the earth, but I would be less of a filth if I could get through this treatment. Polygraphs were difficult, one reason being that when I told the truth, the machine would often record it as a lie, which was quite upsetting to me. Treatment centers use the polygraphs to control you, but many times the guys fail, and when they fail twice in a row, they are kicked out of treatment and are resentenced. One day, while sitting in the waiting room waiting for my rude probation officer, two officers told me to stand up and put my hands behind my back.

"What am I being arrested for? I didn't do anything wrong. Ask my probation officer!"

"She was the one who called," one officer replied.

Come to find out, she was wrong. She had me arrested for an appointment she thought I missed that was scheduled for the following week. I never missed an appointment. Did she apologize for sending me to jail? NO!

A few weeks went by as I was working picking up trash. I began to talk with this lady named Karen. One thing led to another, so I moved from one side of town to the other side to be near her. Her parents helped me when I needed to be secluded, because I had to check in every hour by a phone on a recorded line. My PO allowed me to stay with her parents.

Karen stood by me through most of my treatment. She got to see firsthand how they treated the clients. I eventually moved in with her and proposed to her. She encouraged me to stand up for myself when I was being mistreated. I was fed up with the system and was willing to take my chance in front of the judge. He couldn't extend my sentence.

In class, another guy was having the same problem. We were being taught how to control the very thing that had gotten us into trouble. The system was set up to ignore God, teaching us the textbook method to "recovery," but that didn't work. I had five months remaining on my sentence when this other man stood up and told the therapist that he'd had enough of the abuse.

He decided to take his chances in front of a judge. Like me, he also had an attorney. We were told that if we left, we couldn't come back, and our treatment would not be complete. The next three weeks I continued to work but stopped seeing my PO. When the day arrived to face the judge, my attorney told the judge the situation, along with the DA listening in.

The judge said, "I see here that I can't extend Mr. Gushwa's sentencing to attend another treatment center. So, I will have no choice but to suspend the sentence and make a statement that treatment was not complete. You are to continue to register as a sex offender for the next ten years or until I dismiss you. You must submit a request. Case dismissed."

I was so happy. This was all finished, behind me. Now I could start over. I would show everyone that I could change. I wish I could say how sorry I was to the one I hurt, but I never saw her again.

I knew God was trying to get my attention, yet I was stubborn and unwilling to stop. It's true I learned my lesson about offending, but the thoughts that drove me to my mistakes never went away.

I was permitted to talk to my kids on the phone, but I didn't want to face them in person. I felt dirty inside. I might have gotten by with what I did, but still I knew I had to face that voice that kept telling me to come back because I had no hope of defeating this without Christ. I wanted God to help me but still on my own terms. I never quite got what God was saying to me.

I knew about my salvation. I read about David, Samson, Noah, Paul, and Peter. These men were loved by God despite what they did. Even with all their disobedience, God still stood by their side. Why would I be any different? *I am determined to find out why I am like this. Why do I keep sinning in a sexual way?*

Once again, I decided in my mind that I would make my marriage with Karen work. My daughters were getting impatient with me making excuses for my habits. At first, they were reluctant to come up for Christmas, but after some convincing, they gave in and spent a Christmas with me.

My oldest daughter was married and had two beautiful

daughters. I was proud to be a grandpa, but I was not included much in their lives. This is the consequence you get when you make bad choices. When my girls found out what I had done, they were so angry with me it took years to finally talk with them.

My oldest protected me from my granddaughters. It was one of the worst consequences I could face. My son hadn't talked with me since my youngest daughter graduated from high school. Now he was married with one son. Then he and his wife added two more boys, and that made it three grandsons. I also was protected from them. This only made me hate myself more than ever. I hated my thoughts and my actions. I could never undo what I had done, so why stop?

*I might as well see what else I can get into trouble with. Everybody has turned their backs on me. I still need help. Somebody please stop these thoughts. Why won't you stop them, God?*

*Please, Lord. I can't stand the attacks on my brain anymore. Take them away, God, or I will just continue down this path.*

The first part of my marriage with Karen was pleasant, but every time I saw a teenage girl, my mind began to wander into those dark places again. I would undress them in my mind. *Why not? Isn't that what I have been doing all my life? What's age got to do with it? I like looking at innocent girls. Why not? What's wrong with that? I'm just looking.*

I continued to talk in chat rooms, playing the role of a teenager, but this time I did not try to set them up to meet. I was thrilled just to talk dirty to them. The age didn't matter. I talked to women my age also. If they talked dirty back, then I continued to chat with them. I was fifty-two years old, so I couldn't send my picture. So, what I did was pretend I was a teenage boy for the purpose of getting pictures from them.

I would store them in a folder on the computer so I could send a fake picture of me to them. It was so easy to do. I surfed the web and found partially nude girls, astonished that the web would have such pictures and so many of them. I was angry but also happy that I could look at them.

## My Final Marriage

While I was viewing those pictures, more ads kept popping up of hardcore child pornography. I couldn't believe what I was seeing! While viewing them I kept getting these stronger feelings, but afterward, I felt so ugly and dirty I could hardly stand myself. That's how it had been my entire life, it seemed—back and forth, but never getting enough to quench my thirst for more pornography. I wondered how these pictures could be on the web. It was against the law. These websites were making me more curious than ever. *Why do I wonder so much about why these girls could be on the web? Why do I love to search and stare? Why am I not stopping all this? I keep getting worse. You must think this is funny, God. Why did you ever make me just so I can go through this? If you won't stop this, then kill me!*

I kept repeating such statements to God. In other words, I was daring him. No matter how much pornography was on the computer, I wanted to see more. How could such filth be on the computer? It was to get me to spend money to see more. I never went into these sites unless they were free. I would never pay for them.

I never thought anything would happen to me. I kept this a secret, putting my computer in a separate room so I could

## It Only Takes One Look

chat secretly. Occasionally one of the kids or Karen would pop in, but I figured out how to get out of the chat room quickly. I was so much into chat rooms that when Karen wanted to go do something, I would make up an excuse just to stay home and chat.

Sometimes, I even used this excuse on holidays. Shortly after I began to chat, I started to hate being married. I tried many times to leave, but Karen would block the doorway, wondering what was wrong with me. I told her I hated being married, I wanted to leave, but what I really wanted was sympathy.

Often, I would read in the newspaper about guys getting caught with child pornography on their computers. I found this men's chat room that traded pornography. I believed they would be completely deleted from my hard drive. I lived in a fantasy world looking at the pictures on the websites. This marriage with Karen could have worked, but like my last three, I would make the same mistakes.

I had no respect for anybody, especially God, who I always blamed. When I was upset with my life and hating myself, I would walk out of our home and not come back home for a while. Most of the time, Karen would chase me down or have one of the kids chase me down to tell me to come back home. I wouldn't stop what I was doing on the computer, although I was always scared of getting caught.

I had many warnings to stop or face the consequences. God was speaking very loudly. Many times, I would go on the computer and my stomach would get so upset that I would shake. I knew that sooner or later I would get caught, but that didn't matter anymore. I was driven.

*What if I download pictures on CDs and hide them?* I

thought. *Nobody will ever find them.* Once again, my resourcefulness paid off, or so I thought. I figured out how to transfer pictures to CDs and send them to other guys. So, for months I traded pictures with many men and some women, fathers, and mothers. Months passed. The pictures became so graphic, nothing was left to the imagination.

I wondered how such photos were allowed on the internet. I felt uneasy about the whole thing. I felt very bad looking at them. I wondered how anyone could take pictures of these kids. *Is this what I have become? A father and grandpa looking at pornographic pictures of children. Why?* My heart kept beating faster every time I viewed them. I was torn between getting a thrill over them and feeling convicted. That warning kept coming.

"Stop! Give this addiction to your Lord. He is waiting for you to come back to him. He knows you alone can't stop. He knows every thought and sees everything you are doing. Don't let this continue, because it will only get worse."

For the first time, I knew that God was getting impatient with me. My heart was ripping me apart every time I kept going back. When my convictions got serious, I would stop for a couple of weeks and then go right back to this one chat room. But this time would be my last, I told myself. How did I know that the Lord was going to get my attention in two ways?

First, on my way home from work one afternoon I had an upset wife calling me. "There are four detectives here. They want to know who has this screen name. I don't have it. Do you know who does?"

"Yeah, it's me." My whole body trembled with fear. That consequence had now come. What was I going to do now? I

## It Only Takes One Look

kept driving until the detectives left with my computer. *How did they catch me? I don't have any pictures on my computer. They won't find anything on it. I'm not going to admit to anything unless they have proof.*

I found out later how I was caught. This dad in Florida was sending pictures back and forth to certain guys. When the detectives took his computer, they found pictures that were stored on his hard drive. They found my email on his computer. The sheriff from Florida contacted the sheriff where I lived, and that's when they got the warrant to take my computer. I thought I was cleared until they said that twenty images were on my computer. Apparently, they had the technology to go into my hard drive and produce pictures from echoes. That was it for me.

That day had finally come. I was warned for years to stop, but I hadn't listened. I was too proud to admit that I had a problem. I was so arrogant that I blamed others for my problems. I sat down and thought about how unfair it was for them to search my hard drive.

The next morning Karen was pulled over by the county sheriff's department. The detective told her to call me and have me meet them down the street. When Karen called, I knew what was going on. I told her I would get there as soon as I dressed. It was a Friday morning when I got the call. Karen's mom would bail me out by Monday, so I would at least keep my job. I knew I had to destroy my CDs, so I crushed them up and tried to flush them down the toilet. I never told anyone I had those CDs. After that I took a shower. All I was doing was prolonging going to jail. Then I got another phone call. This time it was the detective.

"If you don't come down here in ten minutes, I will arrest

Karen for having that account. Do you really want me to take your wife to jail?"

"No! I will be there." My first thought was to get in the car and leave. *Get out of the state. Let Karen take the blame. Why should I care? She would get out of it. No! I can't do that. It's my fault. All this is my fault. I will just have to accept what will happen to me. I deserve it.*

I drove down to the flashing lights and got out of my car, where I was handcuffed. Then, I told Karen to bail me out as my head was lowered into the car. My next stop was at the DA's office where I was handcuffed to a table, sitting alone for thirty minutes. When the detective asked me if I wanted to be made a statement, I said no. What was there to say? Whatever I said could be used against me. I didn't want to open myself up for the judge to read it. I was always trying to find a way out.

## A Crack in My Shell

While sitting in that room alone, I had a strange feeling come over me. It was that same soft voice I had heard before telling me, "I love you no matter what."

I turned away from the voice because I was bitter toward God, because now I was a felon with a criminal record waiting to go to jail.

*You happy with that, Lord? If you're not finished, then complete what you're trying to do. Take my life. What purpose do I have now? I'm a loser, no matter how you look at it.* I sobbed in my despair. *Look at me. Look at what I have done. I'm finished. I can't undo this.*

My heart began to open a crack—just enough for the Lord to get my attention. I wasn't convinced that God could help me. I had this vision of God shaking his fist at me, shaking his head in disgust. I knew that I would go to heaven, but I would lose all my rewards. So then why should I care? My life was passing right in front of me.

I looked back at all I had done. I felt the pain I had done to my wives that I had hurt. I could see my young victim having a rough life because of me. How could I ever untangle the mess I was in? Then it hit me. Everything with me began with an "I." My life wasn't about others. It was always about Bob.

God kept that detective out of that room long enough to talk to me. I was told that many hardships would come in the next few years. God was going to draw me close to him. Not yet, though, because something was going to suddenly happen that would put me on my knees. Even then it would take a final year of disaster to draw this stubborn man toward a patient and forgiving God.

The detective walked into the room and told me it was time to take me to booking. While at booking, an officer took my mug shot and fingerprints and then took me to a holding cell where I waited to be put in the central population area. For three days, I looked out the window, thinking of what was about to happen. I would be completely stripped of my freedom.

I'd had all the chances to make a good life for myself. Instead, two days before Christmas, I found myself looking out a window from my cell. *Nobody will visit me. My kids don't care about me. I will never have a chance to see my son.* The next day a cellmate with the same attorney as I had was put into my cell. I tried to witness to him about Christ, but he looked at the cell, then at me, and laughed. It just gave

## How Long, Lord?

me a greater opportunity to tell him that I deserved what I was getting. I finally began to understand that God wasn't the problem. It was me, but I was so full of guilt that it worked more against me while sharing that cell with another man.

The food was no good in jail. So, I gave it to my cellmate. I hated being in there. I caught a glimpse of some of the worst men you could see. I told myself that I shouldn't be in there with all those guys. I didn't know that looking at pictures would get me into so much trouble.

Then my name was called. I was taken to a room with video cameras pointed at the judge. The DA and my attorneys were present. The judge issued me a $25,000 bail, and then I was taken back to a different module with many bunks filled with inmates. There, I waited for Karen and her mom to bail me out. I wondered how many guys were waiting to go to DOC or who would serve their time here in the county jail.

I knew I deserved to be here with them. I had committed so many crimes throughout my life. After hearing my name called finally, I went down to grab my clothes, signed a release form for bond, and walked out the door. I was told to report to the pre-court department for conditions to my release the next day.

When I went home, all I could do was keep silent. All Karen could do was keep asking me how I could ever do what I did. "What next?" she said.

That entire incident occurred over an extended weekend, so to speak, from Friday to Monday. By Tuesday, I was back to work, keeping the weekend adventure to myself. Working kept my mind off the impending court proceedings.

Time kept dragging on and on. It was now 2008, a year after my arrest. According to my attorney, the case looked good. He was trying to get a plea deal to keep me out of jail. I wanted my attorney to fight back because I had never stored any pictures on my computer; they were deleted. Going to my hard drive was desperate.

I kept saying. "So even though I deleted my emails, they can still be produced?"

"Yes, in a criminal case." *If only I knew.*

The case was taking so long to end that I figured I was going to jail, so why not get back on the computer. *What did it matter anymore?* This time, however, I used the web on my phone. When you're in a rut and life seems to be caving in on you, why not just keep going until the bottom falls out? That was a dumb principle to follow.

Six months after I was released on bond and went back to work, I was fired from my job. I was caught sexually harassing a woman at one of the landfills. When I was told to come in to see the district manager, I knew she had told on me. I tried to fight it, but I lost another well-paying job because of my addiction to sexual habits. When I got home, I told Karen it was because of my court case.

## A Knock at the Door

Nothing mattered now. Where would I work now? Thoughts of suicide returned to my mind. *Why live anymore? I can't stay married. I can't beat this addiction. I'm a liar.*

I felt all alone. Losing my grip on anything meaningful, I hated my heart because that was the only thing keeping me alive. It was also the one thing that tore me up inside. I did not dare get a job because my future was so uncertain. Once again, I had to resort to my 401 (K) just for daily needs.

My future was gone. I doubted God was in this mess, but

I was certain that Satan was. He got what he wanted. He tried his best to destroy any kind of relationship I might have had with the Lord.

My attorney was trying to work out a plea deal to put me in a treatment class instead of going to jail. When it was finally completed, I signed forms allowing me to go on work release for six months. With good time, my work release could be reduced. The final verdict was six months on work release and five years in treatment. I had to complete treatment before the judge would release me.

Work release is something like jail. You work during the day and then return to jail at night, for which I was charged a $10 per night bunk fee. I could wear my own personal clothes in jail and bring in my radio and headset. If I violated the terms and conditions of work release, I would be sent upstairs to the regular jail then wait to face the judge.

During my official sentencing, the judge approved the deal my attorney had arranged with the DA. Handcuffed, I was escorted back to booking and to another module where I was assigned a bunk. They allowed me to go home to pick up my clothes within a five-hour window.

With work release, I could use my own car to travel back and forth to a job. I kept my cell phone in my car because every time we checked back into work release, officers inspected our belongings, looking for drugs, cell phones, and any other prohibited items they could confiscate.

Every morning I drove down to the temp services to find temporary work. It was all I could do at that point. I also made money by taking four other guys with me, who each paid me $10 a day.

There was one thing I had to have from home. It was my

Bible. Every Sunday night, I attended church held in the day room. I was embarrassed about my life, but I would not be embarrassed about my faith in Christ. I sometimes looked around and thought, *This is a great place to turn my life around. I am going to read and search the Bible and pray. Maybe this is where the Lord wants me to be.*

Trying to make sense of my life while being in there, I was never embarrassed about guys knowing that I was a Christian. Every chance I had, I took my Bible out and studied it. Many guys would approach me to ask why I was in jail. I knew I couldn't tell them the truth. They would kill me if I did. I began to feel my heart softening up for the Lord. This one verse I memorized as a child came to the front of my mind: "Here I am! I stand at the door and knock. If anyone hears my voice and opens the door, I will come in and eat with that person, and they with me" (Revelation 3:20).

I remembered my grandmother's picture always lit up with Christ standing at the door. I noticed that the door handle was on the inside. That meant I had to open the door. Christ would knock, but he would not force open the door. I had to willingly open the door for him to enter the circumstance of my life.

This meditating on the Lord, with little distractions in my life, led me one afternoon to the dayroom where I dropped to my knees and asked God to change me. I didn't care who came in or if guards saw me. I had hit bottom. I felt like God had busted me, like a father catching his son in the act of disobedience. Nobody would be there for me anymore. I was alone. Then it hit me, like so many other times.

I heard the Lord respond, not in an audible voice, but in a

spiritual sense, saying, "This is where you will begin. These are the types of men you are going to minister to. I am going to send you to them. The difference between you and them is ME. You have had me since you were young, but you didn't have much of me.

"I never walked away from you, Bob. You were never out of my sight. I'm still not done with you. Even though you kept questioning me, I knew your heart. It is time to grow up as a Christian. Your hardship is still not finished yet, but if you will trust in me, I will use you in a wondrous way."

Weeping, I continued to hear him say: "It's time for you to be tested. It's time for you to listen to me. The world around you will get much worse, but if you abide in me, I will protect you. I haven't lost control of you, nor the world. My love for you has never changed. No sin is too big that I couldn't love you. No matter how much you disrespected me, I still loved you. I also love the men who are around you. Those you meet, tell them that I love them and that I will forgive their sins.

"You are going to experience what it's like to be the victim, but I will always be there for you. When I am finished teaching and testing you, then I will use you."

I was scared, not knowing what exactly he meant, but I was sure he meant it. I had picked out a table so the guys would always know where I was sitting and could see me reading my Bible. Often some would come and talk with me. It was my favorite table sitting close to the hot water pot, which I always kept full for the guys. Many guys would make fun of me, but I would just walk away.

"Hey you! Your God is dead. No such thing as a God. If there's a God, why are you in here then?" some would shout.

"I guess you will find out if he is dead, but will it be too late for you?" I would respond.

"Are you saying that I'm going to hell?"

"I never said that. Only God judges the unsaved. Which one are you?"

"Hey, preacher man, why are you in here then? I guess your God didn't much help you, man," they mocked.

"I put myself in here. I can't blame God for my actions. I decided to disobey him. Now look where I'm at. But I won't go to hell."

"We all are in hell," they would say, giggling.

I managed to keep my bills paid at the jail and still ordered things from the commissary. I either resold them to guys who couldn't buy them or gave them away. I tried to stay away from meals, often giving mine away.

Meanwhile, thinking of my life outside of work release and prayer time in the day room, I knew that Karen was going to file papers for divorce, so when that day came, I wasn't shocked. What did shock me, however, was that she wouldn't go away. She stood there by my side.

Karen was my fourth wife, my fourth failed marriage. I told myself I would never get married again. Many of my friends would tell me that someone would come along eventually, but I would just shake it off. With four chances at marriage, I had made a mess out of them all.

Still today, as I write this, the hardest marriage that I could not shake was the one with Sue—the one woman I had truly loved, but I had allowed selfish desires to ruin our lives. I am not sure I will ever get over what I did to her and our family. I try to imagine the one great upside to all these wives is that one day I will see them again in heaven. There, we will not reminisce of things done on earth. Just to know they will be there puts a smile on my face. Do I think of them? Yes! Do I pray for them? All the time.

What happened next in my journey from bondage to freedom was a shock to my whole personal life. It was the true beginning of my spiritual growth—the knowledge of who God truly is.

## Thirteen

# Death of a Son

The next two trials were going to teach me lessons. These trials would teach me how Jesus cared for me. And though life would continue to present challenges, temptations, and a few more tests, these two trials changed me more than any others preceding them or to this day.

The first of these trials happened when I had only two weeks left on my work release sentence. My youngest daughter had told me that my son Mike wanted to see me after I got out. I hadn't talked with my son for almost eighteen years, not since he had gotten married. Hearing the news that he wanted to see me brought me great joy. I was finally going to get a chance to reconcile with him, to put to rest our differences.

I knew that I wasn't the father I should have been in his life. I wanted to face him, man to man, to tell him how deeply sorry I was for misbehaving as his father. I thought of how wonderful it would be to hug my son after all these years and how maybe, someday, I could go fishing with my son and my grandsons. *I've waited all these years. Finally! I can throw all this away and start over.*

Counting down the days for his visit came to a sudden, dreadful end when my daughter called Karen, telling her to find me immediately, make me stop what I was doing, and to tell me that she had to talk to me. As I was driving back to jail from work, Karen called and relayed the important message.

"OK. Meet me in the parking lot of the jail."

It had been a great, full day at work. My life was beginning to feel different, in a good way. I was healing and growing in the Lord, and today was one day closer to seeing my son. As I was getting out of the car, Karen said, "You need to sit down before I get your daughter on the phone."

"Dad," my daughter said, "I have some bad news for you. Mike was found dead in his bedroom. He was found reaching for the phone. They found him at ten thirty this morning. I will let you know when the funeral will be."

I sat there in tears not saying a word. I knew this was one of the consequences I had to face because of my disobedience. *But not this, God. Don't take Mike! This isn't fair, God. You allowed me to go through so much turbulence and now you take my only son. That's not fair, God.* Weeping, I thought, *God, you didn't even give me a chance to tell Mike how sorry I was!*

"Dad," my daughter said, bringing me back to attention, "are you there? I can hear you crying. I'm so sorry, Dad, but you still have us girls. Don't forget that."

"I know. This is my fault that he died. If I wasn't so selfish with my reckless life, maybe Mike would still be alive, but no. I had to act this way. It's all my fault. Now I have no son to reconcile with."

After I hung up the phone, I walked in a daze back inside the jail. The deputy asked me if I was all right. With my head feeling lower than my feet, I replied, "No. My son died."

"I'm so sorry," the deputy consoled me. "Where is the funeral going to be held?"

"Colorado Springs."

"I will talk to the sergeant in charge on that day and see if we can give you a day's pass to attend his funeral."

When the chaplain came to visit me, I told him how bad I felt about not being able to tell Mike how sorry I was. He suggested I write a letter to my son and put it under his hands at the funeral. "You can bury it with him then," he said. Thinking it was a great idea, I took to writing the letter to my son.

Soon, the deputy returned to me, saying, "The sergeant said it would be OK for you to go to Colorado Springs. Here is your pass. You must be back by nine p.m. This should give you a little more time to be with your family. Once again, I'm so sorry for your loss. I've been where you're at."

"How's that?"

"I lost my son too. He killed himself about eight years ago."

"How long did it take you to get over it?"

"You never really get over it. I think about my son almost every day. I wonder what he would look like if he were still alive. You just always wonder. It never goes away. You must learn how to deal with it. As time passes, it gets a little easier, but it never totally goes away."

"Thanks for sharing that with me," I expressed with sincere gratitude. He didn't have to say anything, but hearing that from him did help me a bit. Still, the rest of the day, I laid in my bunk telling myself that it was all my fault, though I knew that the Lord had his hand in this. Lying in my bunk, I could feel the hand of the Lord on my back, and a chill went through me like cold ice. There was no one else in the area.

"I am the God that you have turned your back on. This is trial number one. What will you do with this, Bob? I am the

God of all creation. I give and I take. I gave you a son, and now I took your son. I never asked you how, when, or why Mike was going to die. The attitude that you have toward me is dishonoring. Will you blame me for Mike's death, or will you thank me?"

"Oh yes, Lord," I spoke aloud with bitterness and sarcasm dripping from my tongue. "I'm going to thank you for killing my only son. I feel like you set me up to fall. You could have at least let me see and talk to Mike. Sure, I get to see him now. DEAD!"

My words of disrespect toward the Lord weren't coming from my heart. In my heart, I knew I was wrong. I just wanted someone to blame other than myself. I had backslidden so far from God that I didn't want to see myself as a failure. Everything around me was falling apart. I knew the time was getting terribly close for God to really get my attention. If Mike's death didn't get it, nothing would.

Karen volunteered to pick me up and take me to the funeral. Walking into the church, my stomach felt like a washing machine, twisting, turning, spinning, with jolting pain and discomfort throughout my whole body. I saw Mike's casket in a distance along the altar railings.

Continuing to walk into the sanctuary, I saw pictures of Mike growing up with Sue and me. I couldn't take a step closer. Guilt overwhelmed me. I could not face him. That was my little boy in there. He was the only son I had. Regrets, guilt, and shame were tearing me up.

I heard my youngest daughter say, "Dad, you need to go down there alone and say goodbye to Mike."

Shaking my drooping head, I cried, "I can't go down there. I just want to leave."

"I will walk down there with you, and then I'll leave you two alone."

I finally stood in front of Mike. My daughter let go of my arm and slowly walked away, leaving me alone with my dead son. I slipped my envelope underneath Mike's hands and stood there crying. I don't know how I was breathing at that moment. My will to live was lower than it had ever been. My sense for living was there in the casket. Two weeks later, I would have been talking to a living boy, my son. Now I stared at him, no life in him, and none left in me either.

*Okay, God, here I am. You want my attention. Here I am. Why not me? Why don't you take me instead of Mike? Mike has three sons. What about them? Who will raise them, Lord? Why Mike? Don't let me take the blame for this. Don't use Mike to get my attention.* I sobbed. *It is me you want. Raise him up and take me. I'm at fault.*

"I want you to listen to me, Bob," I felt the Lord say. "I am the God of the living and of the dead. Although your son looks dead lying there, he is not. He is alive with me. I give and I take. You have no authority over me, Bob. I will do what will please me. Though your son is dead, he is alive. You must go on, because I'm not finished with you yet."

"Did you take my son to get my attention? Why didn't you allow me to see my son? I would have made it right."

"But you wouldn't make that change. I waited for you to give this lifestyle up, but you wouldn't let go. I want you to bury your son, grieve for a short time, and then stand ready to listen to me. You will go through one more trial. This one will get your attention. I will teach you and use you to further my purpose. Remember, Bob, I love Mike, and I love you."

I knew that I was the reason my son was lying there, but

what could I do now? It was too late. In my heart, I knew what I had to do. As my son was lying there, I knelt at the altar next to his casket and told the Lord that I was so sorry for my life. I made some promises to him, at least one of which I kept—to read the Bible in its entirety from Genesis through Revelation.

As I knelt there, I felt the presence of the Holy Spirit upon me, telling me that God was going to use me. All I knew for sure at the time was that my actions had put my son in the grave. Still, I continued to beg and wrestle with the Lord.

*Is this what it took for you to get my attention? Why couldn't you do it in a different way? Who will raise my grandsons? Will this end now? Will I be the next to go? I'm the one that deserves to die, not Mike. Mike has a family. I have nobody. Oh God, why have you allowed me to do all the wicked sins against you, and still here I am?*

*I beg of you, God, please take this from me. I can't manage my life anymore. I can't go through another treatment class again. I know what the truth is. My problem is you won't help me live the truth. Why not?*

*Why do I keep making the mistakes I hate doing? I must stop now. Right now. Here at the altar. Don't let me continue going on like this. Why won't you tell me why you're doing this to me? Why, God?*

Sobbing at the altar, I waited to hear from the Lord, but I heard nothing. At that moment, I felt betrayed by God. I took his silence to mean that truly I was to blame for Mike's death. My daughters helped me get up. Looking around, watching the space between Mike and me get farther apart with every step I took, I thought, again, *This is all my fault.*

During the service, slides of our children displayed on the screen reminded me of how much I longed to start over with Sue and the kids. I wanted to tell Sue how sorry I was about everything, but she walked away. I felt so out of place. My head was spinning. In front of me, my whole life seemed to pass me by. I searched my mind for someone who would love me.

Apparently, my ex-wives didn't, my kids didn't. My grandsons didn't know me. Mike's wife was holding grudges. I was still being put down day after day. I tried to change, but I wasn't accepted.

*So, why change then? If no one will give me a chance, then I will just be like I have always been. A bunch of nothing.*

I have never sat down and talked with Sue since the day I took the kids and left the house. Many of you know what I'm talking about. You make a mess of your life, but no one will give you a chance to turn around, and when you do, you're still considered the same old person with the same mistakes hanging over your head. That's unfair, especially when someone works hard to make changes in his or her life.

After the funeral, I returned to jail, to my world of nothing, and just laid on my bunk thinking about my son and my grandsons. *God betrayed me again!* Deep down, though, I had experienced enough of God to know I was wrong about him.

Two weeks to go in work release and then I would be released for good, except for the five years of probation and treatment I would have to endure. What lay ahead of me I did not know, but time would soon unravel itself through polygraphs, failures, and more trials. I knew I had to keep my nose clean.

## Death of a Son

In those remaining two weeks of work release, I poured out my heart to the Lord. Alone, I would go in the day room to kneel and pray. I didn't care if the deputies or inmates came in. I was hurting from the loss of my son, and I felt that God was walking away from me. I knew that Mike was safe in heaven, but God walking away from me scared me.

I began to make good on my promise to God to read the Bible right after I got out of jail. When I started reading about David, I felt a little encouraged because I learned that God always loved him despite his failures. When David lost his son because of his sin with Bathsheba, I thought about my sin with Sue. I also lost my son. This verse spoke to me: "But now that he is dead, why should I go on fasting? Can I bring him back again? I will go to him, but he will not return to me" (2 Samuel 12:23).

David had Uriah killed to cover up his sin with Bathsheba. The Lord spared the lives of both David and Bathsheba, but the Lord took their son's life. I felt this was what God had done to me. Sure, I would never have another son to build a temple, nor another son to hunt me down to take my life, but I found a familiarity with the story of David that helped me. I too lost my son because of my sexual sins. Sexual sins were rampant in the Bible.

As I continued my reading through God's Word, I finally didn't feel as alone as I once did, although I still felt guilty. I had no one. I couldn't go out in the community whenever I wanted to. I had to account for the time I spent in certain places. Church was out of the question, and talking about God in class was frowned upon and even silenced at times. The other ten guys in our class knew that I was a Christian. What I believed in would contradict what was being taught by the therapist, whom I often questioned. She couldn't explain why my habits and my Christianity contradicted each other. Thankfully, I was beginning to see that the problem was me, although much more clarity would be needed for me to finally understand it in my heart.

I still felt like God was allowing me to go through this, but why? Throughout those five years of treatment, I lived in fear and with threats. I just wanted to get out of there. I didn't want to learn anything from those therapists. They were teaching me principles and concepts contrary to the Word of God, which made me feel uneasy in class. During this time, however, I did have time to think about where I stood with God, which was good for me to learn.

Treatment centers can be problematic. I was being taught how to cope with the one thing that got me into trouble rather than ridding it from my life. They teach you that lust in the right way is acceptable. When it comes down to objectification, they contradict themselves. I used to get in arguments with the other guys, who would laugh at me. I guess I did have values after all! I wish I would have relied on them earlier in life. Now I was suddenly standing up for what is right, but why now?

There are so many things I can't explain, but I know that God has always had a hand in my life. Going through treatment, after the loss of my son, I found myself hungry for more from God. Hidden in my heart was the truth about sexuality. I had known before I sinned that what I was about to do would be disobedient to God and my family. I knew sooner or later I would find myself in some treatment center somewhere. I knew sooner or later I would get caught. How? Because the voice of the Holy Spirit was always speaking in my heart. I felt so wrong inside. While I did wrong on the outside, something was always stirring inside. I knew what it was, but I didn't want to acknowledge it because then I would have to quit what brought me pleasure.

God placed in my life a great probation officer. I believe God specially assigned him to be able to handle me and my stubborn ways. My probation officer became the only person in the world I really had, someone I could open to. He was patient with me when I made mistakes. I am thankful for him.

I was given permission to stay with Karen for one night, and then I had to find a place of my own. When that night came, I couldn't sleep. When the clock struck midnight, I walked through the jail doors alone. No cheers. Just a quiet walk out to the fresh air. I walked to my car and went to Karen's house. I had saved money for a deposit on an apartment. The next day I secured a one-bedroom apartment and a job working through a temp service driving cars at an auction.

I had to figure out how to get through the next five years. I was lost at what to do to keep myself from repeating my sins. I thought I had tried everything to quit, but still I kept going back to my habit. I had prayed for years that the Lord would take the evil desires from me. I wanted a quick fix from God. I wanted to go to bed and wake up the next day cured. That didn't happen, so I was disappointed with God. So, once again, I gave up and went back to my old sinful habits.

I want to say again, I always knew I was saved, but sometimes in doubt, I would try to remind God that we had a deal. I had given my life to him, and he would save me from hell. But that was it. It's hard to try to be a good Christian when you're constantly being annoyed by the devil. I'm a stubborn man, so God was going to have to use whatever it took to change my life.

## Fourteen

# Probation and Treatment

### Journey to Freedom

I might have been free from jail, but I was still miserable inside. I had hurt the ones who put their trust in me and was still feeling the guilt. Treatment taught us about empathy, something I thought might be helpful for me to learn. We wrote letters to our victims, telling them how sorry we were, taking full responsibility for our actions. But I didn't know my victim's address.

When I first went to class, I felt so small because I knew that Jesus was the answer, and this treatment program was a waste of my time. *I know where I need to get my answers. I shouldn't even be here.* I had known better than to do what I had done in my past.

God had given me ample warning to give up this addiction. But I didn't want to listen. So now, I had to listen to the secular answers taught to sex offenders by the justice system. I knew that what they taught was a temporary solution. God had the permanent answer. All I had to do was ask the Lord for it.

I was still reading the Bible from Genesis to Revelation in search of answers to understand more of why I chose to live the wicked life of my past. I knew that figuring things out wouldn't be easy because the past was still haunting me.

Every day I kept thinking about the mistakes I had made. They were numerous. How could I ever get close to God?

*If I know better than God, then why am I sitting in this chair at treatment waiting for the therapist to come in? I must figure out how to skate through this class. Look at these guys all staring at me. I wonder what they did. I wonder how long they have been in here. I'm the newbie now.*

Here I was, the first day. Two therapists walked in, smiling.

"Hello there, Bob. Welcome to our class. I want each member to go around and say their name, what you're in here for, and how long you've been in here."

One classmate began, "Hi! My name is Jim. I molested my next-door neighbor. She was twelve. I have been in here for six years. Just do as you're told and keep the rules, and you will graduate."

I should have left a year earlier, but the judge had extended so I could finish. I violated some rules. I sat there with a smirk on my face. Everyone in the class could tell I was smart talking. I thought every one of those guys were nuts.

Back when I was making bad decisions in my life, I didn't think God would allow me to end up here. He had warned me many times, but I didn't think that God would go through with it. I knew the verses that talked about how loving and merciful God was, how he would keep me safe from all harm. I ignored all the ones that spoke of obedience and justice and fellowship. I couldn't argue with God, not that any of us really wins, but I didn't like where I was and what I was having to deal with.

## Realization

During those five years, I learned a lot about the war on men's minds. I found myself defending righteous living. Sometimes while driving home after leaving class, I would be astonished at how I was so against the life I had formerly thought was mine to live.

The secular teachings in treatment class made me realize that those sexual habits that were destroying lives were being tolerated and even encouraged by society at large. The more I came to class and listened to answers that didn't help me spiritually, the more turned off I was. I became tone deaf to what they were saying and more open to hearing what the Word of God had to say. Continuing to read the Bible, I learned of many men and women who fell into sexual temptations. It helped me to recognize some things about what I had struggled with my whole life. I finally was beginning to understand that I wasn't alone. Not that I was happy they or I fell into sin, but it encouraged me to know for once I wasn't alone. I compared my life to their lives. Some guys would come to God soon after they were caught, but I was persistently running away from him.

Here I was, knowledge being poured into me by secular teaching and by divine teaching. Which would I accept? Which one would I live by? I could accept the government's answers to sexual crimes or accept what God says about sexual sins. I would have to take a stand. I had to choose one way or the other. I could no longer straddle the fence.

It was true that I had gone through a long period of time hurting people. Too selfish to think of others, I thought only about myself, satisfying my own desires, often feeling sorry for myself. Now this was going to change. I didn't know how

God was going to do it. I feared the other test I recalled that God had said I would have to face. *Could this treatment be the last big test?*

The first half of treatment, I mostly kept quiet and failed the polygraphs. I always tried to keep the rules, but when I failed polygraphs for telling the truth, it made me bitter. It cost me $250 every time I took them. Everything cost money—treatment, polygraphs, court fines, and my living expenses.

During the last three years in treatment was when I began to really call upon the Lord. At first it was about him getting me out of treatment or making people pay for mistreatment in classes. We were told never to keep secrets, but I still did. I couldn't talk to a woman therapist about objectification, sexual thoughts, or men's problems. It didn't seem right, and it certainly wouldn't make me any better.

One of the rules that treatment had was to always have one man and one woman in group therapy. That never happened. We always had women. Many times, the women didn't understand questions from us. Treatment was not for the weak. I have watched guys walk in and out the doors. If you don't keep the rules, treatment centers will manipulate, threaten, and send you to other classes. They will make you take a monthly polygraph. All this costs money. The person going through treatment most likely will lose his family because most of his money goes toward treatment costs.

Also, throughout the process of treatment, you can experience drastic mood changes, which can be good or bad. You have to learn to be strong through the trials that inevitably come. I know that most centers think they are doing what's best for the clients, but when the offender gets out, he will most always remember the treatment received as demeaning and destructive. It's hard to get over those feelings, especially when most offenders come from a lifetime of negative feelings, which play a big role in their behavior patterns in the first place. You will also financially pay for what you have done.

I remember that I had a string of failures when taking the polygraph. I was angry when I told the truth but still failed. The therapists made me move out of my apartment into this SLA (shared living arrangement). Mine was a house divided in half, with two guys living on one side, and two others living on the other side. We had to be responsible for each other. I hated every second I was in there. Another treatment center oversaw the house. In order to get out, I had to pass two polygraphs. I spent eighteen months in that house.

My roommate was also a Christian, which was the only good thing about the place. We knew that our disobedience to God had put us in there, and we were determined not to let those in charge tear us down. He and I both applied for the same job and were hired. We managed to keep our jobs and stay caught up on our bills, two signs of healthy functioning, according to the treatment's centers. Nevertheless, the pointing of fingers and accusing us of violating the rules were everyday occurrences.

## The Cost of Recovery

Once a week I attended my class. One of the rules was not keeping secrets from the class. Here we were—all guys—with two female therapists. It was hard to discuss with women the problems that men bear every day. The therapist admitted that there were some things they couldn't understand, but if we wanted to meet with the director (a male) one-on-one, then we had to make an appointment. (That would also cost extra.)

"You're keeping God out of this. I won't let you tell me what to think. You're wrong telling me to cut down on the God stuff. You people are nuts. I can't change my sexual habits if you're telling me that I can keep some of them."

The cost of treatment was becoming a burden. Every time I thought I was catching up, I got behind and then had to work hard to catch up again. Many guys couldn't find a job because of their backgrounds. The Lord blessed me by providing me with steady employment.

During the last three months of SLA, I was talking on the phone with a lady named Kim that I lived next door to in the apartment prior to moving to the SLA. Sometimes she would come over to visit and talk for a while. She said she was living with a guy who mistreated her. *Hmmm.* What did I do? I convinced her to move in with me after I got out.

Although she and I had agreed to move in together, the treatment class and the therapist disagreed. Of course, I didn't care what they said. There was a woman involved here, and I would do what I felt like doing. Just like before, I made another big mistake. I remembered what the Lord said about a final major test

"I am rescuing her from this abusive guy." I tried to explain this to the class, but they wouldn't listen.

Sometimes you never learn about a person until it's too late. This would be the last lesson that would finally get my attention. I let her live in a room. I explained to her that she could be my roommate, but if my PO came over for a visit in the evening, she would have to say that she was just visiting.

That never did happen. Every time he came over, he called me up on my cell phone and told me to open the back door and wave. Things were going well between us, but little by little I was learning who she really was and how out of God's will I was once again.

I kept reading through the Bible, and what great messages I was getting! My heart was being filled with the truth. The battle with Satan was intense, but I was getting closer to the Lord even though I had many questions while reading. I listened to Christian broadcasting, which was making me think more and more about who I truly was in the sight of God. I continued to wage the war between my feelings and guilt.

Kim had a problem with taking Ambien to fall asleep. She could take four at a time, sleep, eat, watch TV, and go back to bed. She slept during the day and stayed up at night. While I was sleeping, she would sneak guys over. Sometimes I knew about them and turned my head. At first it gave me a thrill to know and see her with these guys. But day after day I was getting sick of all this.

Her male friends were weird, all with stories of mayhem, trouble, and violence. One guy stole meat from a grocery store, then resold it. Sometimes he would come over and visit her. That was fine until I caught them together. I was angry but curious. One part of me was so angry because this was my home, while the other part got a thrill out of it. I knew I should try to do something about it. I had to keep the guy from coming over because I was being torn apart inside. I called up his dad and told him to come over and get his son. I told him to never come back.

God was trying to show me what kind of person I had become over the past forty-four years. At first, I didn't understand how I could be compared to a thief and a man who uses women, but the Holy Spirit has a way of speaking to my heart and mind. At this point, I was ready to hear what the Spirit would say. "This is what you have become. You have stolen from the ones who loved you. You stole their identity; you stole their innocence. These people in your past didn't deserve what you did to them. This is not who you are in Christ.

"You will learn what your identity is and who gives it to you. Your life will change if you let me help you. Look around you, Bob. You're not happy because of the lifestyle you keep choosing to live. You have always known that it was wrong, but you chose to go your own way. This test will end soon, but I will let you choose how it ends."

Hearing this scared me. My God was right; I knew in my heart that sexual sins were destroying me. Before I committed them, my body would react, but I still did them anyway. After hearing the Spirit speak to me, I knew I had to make changes.

I set up rules in my home. I told my roommate no more of this lying around in my home with guys. One day, she had this couple over that she met when she stayed in a motel. The guy was a panhandler, a shoplifter, suicidal, and had this affection toward my roommate.

When I arrived home from work, I heard this noise in her room, so I slipped upstairs and found the two of them together. I told him to leave, which he did, and then she began yelling at me, "I can have anybody I want in this room, and you can't stop me. It's my room."

A week later, she did it again. She brought that same guy back. But this time he was drinking liquor and smoking marijuana. Sitting in my chair downstairs, seething with anger yet fearful of the consequences from God, I had hit rock bottom.

My landlord told me that Kim was still on the lease, so there had to be a good reason to evict her. I tried to convince my landlord of the drugs, but the neighbors never smelled it, so she didn't believe me. Then, I tried to convince Kim to move away with this guy.

I was in the middle of a mess. To make matters worse, the guy's girlfriend found out about him and came storming over to start a ruckus. I called the cops to have him taken off the property. Still, the guy continued to call on Kim.

## Mirror to the Past

I figured if she was going to act this way, I would start to charge her rent. Every month I received a small payment. I didn't know this would backfire, but when Kim told me that she was half partner of my apartment, I knew I had to get rid of her. Her life was on a collision course, but so was mine. I wanted to pick up my pieces, not hers.

God was showing me how I had gotten here. He reminded me how such a small sin led to this lifestyle. Of course, I reminded God how many times I had asked him to remove my desires, the temptations, the circumstances. I was angry at him, but all along God was pouring out his love. Those things that brought a rush to my body were beginning to fade away. *Why now? Why not back then?*

Day after day, this guy would sneak in, and then I would have to call the cops when he got so drunk, he couldn't stand up. He fell into my furniture and started bleeding. I opened the door and told him to get lost and not to come back.

Kim continued to bring trouble into my apartment. I

would be sleeping and wake up to noise, then go back to bed. I didn't know what to do. I was being used, blackmailed, and threatened in my own home. This guy, who I will call Roger, and his girlfriend were always in trouble, but Kim acted like she was the innocent victim. Like a police officer said to me, "It's Kim's fault. She is the one who keeps letting him in."

I figured I would charge him for rent also. I would go after their money and maybe they would leave. Like always, that strategy backfired too. Roger would be nice one day, then go out to get high, come back to my apartment, and get Kim drunk. I would not join them because I wanted to change. I knew I was slipping so far back that I could sense God putting me on a shelf and letting me be a part of this mess.

Finally, one day, I woke up sick. My heart, my mind, and my body were at their lowest. I couldn't get rid of Kim and Roger, and I knew that my life had to change once and for all. But how? How was I going to change my style of living?

Then I heard the voice of the Lord again, "You always had the choice to make the right decisions. But without me, you can do nothing. *Nothing* is where you're at, Bob. In your last forty-four years, what have you gained by the pleasures of this world? Do you have the power to change your life? Do you know what to do? Do you want to continue making your own decisions? Do you trust in yourself to change?"

He was right. My life was a mess. My heart had always been soft for people, but I had used my concern for people so I could gratify myself. My heart was hurting for Kim, because I was seeing some familiarity in her: ME! The things she was doing to me, I had done to others. She and Roger were a mirror to my face.

Crying out to the Lord, I began to acknowledge that he had always been there. No matter what I had done, he had never let go. I was reading the right words in the Bible at the right time in my life. How could this be happening to me? What would help me get away from this situation?

In the meantime, Roger started bringing over another friend. Next thing I knew, they were drunk and fighting over Kim. I called the cops for the fourth time, and finally, both guys were taken to detox. When Kim was sleeping, I looked through her cell phone to find her son's cell phone number. He lived in Houston. I told him the situation, that she needed to get down there with her family. He knew where Kim could stay.

The next day I convinced Kim that she needed to get away from all this and move back to Houston. I would split the cost of renting a pickup truck. I was willing to drive her down there, but then she added a kink in my plans. She convinced Roger to go with her down to Houston.

When Roger's girlfriend heard about this, the cat fights broke out. Three days before I was to take them to Houston, while Kim was upstairs sleeping, Roger took a knife and cut his wrist. I was at work when all this happened. After he cut himself, he yelled at Kim to come downstairs.

Blood was staining the carpet and dripping onto the kitchen floor. Kim convinced him to go to the coffee shop and call an ambulance. Then, the police once again showed up to talk with Kim. They asked where I was. She said I was at work. I heard about all this when I got home to find Roger's friend there watching TV with Kim.

"Kim, I called your son," I said. "We are leaving in two days. That's final! No more discussion." I finally put my foot down. I was beginning to fight for my own life, as if it meant something to me for the first time in my life. I didn't know how I was going to do it, nor did I care how, but I was going to trust the Lord. I just was so sick of myself.

The night before we were going to leave for Houston, I found Roger getting beat up by his friend. I broke it up and called the cops, who chased down his friend and then took him to jail. The next day finally arrived. With a packed truck and no more obstacles in our path, we left for Houston. I drove nonstop except for gas.

Once we arrived, Roger unpacked the pickup, and I was ready to roll out of there, leaving behind the mess they had brought into my life. I just wanted to get away from that place. I didn't get five blocks away when Kim called me. "You need to come back and get Roger. He can't stay here. My son thinks he is nuts and will not allow him to stay. You need to take him back."

I was not happy, but I went back and got Roger. I told him just to shut up and sleep or he could take the bus back. That was the last time I ever saw Kim. On the ride back I tried to talk to Roger about leaving Kim alone and starting over with his other girlfriend. Dropping him off at a close relative's house was the last time I ever saw him.

## Repentance

As a child of the Lord, I felt like I was going to get a scolding about what had happened in my life. I was expecting harsh, mean words from God and the ceiling to fall on me. When I arrived back home, I sat in the truck staring at where I lived. I pictured the mess I had brought upon myself, knowing there was no one to blame but myself. As I walked into my living room, I felt a sense of relief; the huge final test was complete.

Here I stood in my living room with broken furniture, and all I could do was kneel at my sofa and cry into my pillow over the wasted life I had lived. What could I do now? I felt so useless, so guilty. Memories from the past forty-four years came rushing through my mind. I couldn't live with this guilt, this shame. Remorse for all that I had done came out as tears flowing down my cheeks.

Then, in that mess of a home, in my most vulnerable, open position, the strangest thing happened. I felt the presence of the Lord there with his hands on my shoulders. I could not move. He wasn't a grumpy old man who was going to make me pay for my sins. It was a loving Father, there to comfort me. I felt this peace come over my body. I kept crying out to God, "Please don't abandon me. Not now. I have no one. I need you."

Before I got off my knees, I told the Lord that I would try to be obedient to him. I confessed I knew what I had done was sinful. I would trust in him. I didn't know how or what he was going to do, but I had this feeling that God was going to use my life. "Lord, I come to you and say that I'm so sorry for the past life I lived. I know that you remember every thought and deed I did. I can't even remember all that I did, but you do. I don't know why you're still here and why I'm so important to you. I don't feel that way. I know that I have disappointed you, and I am so sorry.

"I can't manage my life from here on out. I hate what immorality has done to me. In your name, forgive me for all the immoral behaviors. I have always known they were wrong. I want to fight against pornography and abuse. I know that you died on the cross for every sin. I know that your grace and mercy have covered my mistakes.

"I don't understand why I did this, but I trust you will begin a new start with me. I want no other. I have lived what Satan offered me, and now I reject it. Use me, Lord. Use this sinner who is saved by grace. Change my heart. I have opened it up for you to come in. Draw me close because I'm scared. I have been wandering around for so long, and people have suffered because of me."

I felt my Savior say, "I have always loved you. You have always been my child. You're not alone. You have read in the Bible that many men were caught in the same sins you were. However, I still loved them, and they came back to me. I blessed them, and now they are your examples.

"If you trust in me and do as I say, you will be blessed. The memories and scars will still be there, but I will help you manage them. I am going to teach you deep, meaningful life that you can live. You stand by my side and watch what I will do with your life.

"I get the glory of what you have done. I change lives. Now live it and tell what I have done for you. Love me, stand with me. Don't ever let go of me. Remember what happens when you do. I will bless you, Bob, when you obey me."

There it is—my story. Not a proud one, I admit. I still sometimes ask myself, like many of you, "How could I have ever gotten caught in this trap? Why did I continue doing it? Why did it take God so long to answer my prayers?"

Our country is going down the wrong road because we accept sinful sexuality as normal. What seems to be normal is disobedience to God. So many have taken God out of the picture. When you do this, you let yourself and others control what's right or wrong, according to who?

I would really like to get down to this question: Who is right, God or man? One or the other is telling the truth. It can't be both. If man is right, then God is irrelevant; and if God is irrelevant, then he ceases to be God. Yet, he is our creator. Then all of existence will cease because the Creator will have let us down. Keep this in mind as we continue to look at the mess man has made when we tried to change a God who says that he changes not.

> *They will perish, but you remain; they will all wear out like a garment. You will roll them up like a robe; like a garment they will be changed. But you remain the same, and your years will never end* (Hebrews 1:11–12).

> *For I the LORD do not change* (Malachi 3:6 ESV).

So, what is the truth about your normal lifestyle? What is the lie? One thing most people don't want to hear is the truth because truth may hurt or cause a change. One thing truth does is it goes straight to the heart, and most people's hearts have turned cold.

Social media can't get it right, politicians hardly get it right, and talk shows don't talk about the truth. These groups, these systems build up more hatred. So, what is the truth? The truth does not come from man's perception.

Many worship dead men. Why worship someone still in the grave? They have no truth. Truth is not found in death but rather in life. Throughout my forty-four years in sexual sin, I always knew what the truth was. I just never wanted to follow and obey it. I wanted to play the truth in church, then live the lie in the streets.

If you're a born-again Christian living in sexual sins, you

know in your heart that it's wrong. Maybe, you feel you can't let go, or maybe you're like I was—you just *won't* let go. I understand how difficult that is. We get mindsets thinking that sin is natural.

## What Is the Truth?

We live in a culture that doesn't want to hear the truth, although many people somehow live according to someone's truth. Whether that someone be a pop star or athlete, people want to continue living according to what others say is right. But I have two questions to ask you:

1. So far, how is that lie working out for you?
2. Are the opinions of others helping you in your personal life? Do you live by what others say?

We live every day with news, talk shows, newspapers, and politicians telling us how to live. Then they help us align with their views. Politicians pass laws to make us live by their views. More and more we are losing our freedoms.

Sadly, our government has wasted the last fifty years setting standards for people to live by, not morally, but immorally, and we have accepted their views as truth. Because of this, our country is being detached from the very heart of its birth—biblical principles and standards, our Christian heritage. Changes don't happen overnight, but has our country tried to make a moral change? I don't believe so.

I have never seen such a perilous country, just waiting to lose its blessings from the God they once served. Thanks be to God, we do have some churches who stand up for truth.

Who will dare to stand up and oppose the laws that shake their fist at our Creator? It seems that man has no fear, that is, respect for God, unless there is a tragedy or national crisis. Then the people call out to God; but as things get better, they go back to their normal lives and forget about the God for whom they cried out for in distress—until the next one.

We could avoid so many tragedies if we would just obey God and turn our lives over to him. This is what I have done, but each person has their own choice, their own free will. You too have a choice. You can take a chance and see what's down the road as you continue to live immorally with pornography in your life. Know this, however: There is a dead end somewhere. When and where is up to God.

Many say to me, "By who's truth do I believe? YOURS?"

I hear this almost every time I have a chance to voice my faith. My faith is the truth spoken by God through his Word, the Bible. Once again, I hear, "It's just a book that some guys wrote."

It is impossible to write the Bible without the inspiration of the Holy Spirit. Its content is so consistent about man and sin, and the love of God to save us through Jesus Christ. Only God could pull that off. The prophecies alone have been accurate up to this day.

Consider for a moment how pitiful it is to live apart from God. You have made it this far living your way. You know you deserve the consequences of your lifestyle because you failed to be obedient. After all, Satan will always take you back if you decide to reject Christ.

## A Spark

All it took was a spark, only one look to get my attention. I could have thrown the magazines out, but every time I kept those magazines when I was a child, the spark was kept lit. That's the way it is with sin.

## It Only Takes One Look

*It's just an innocent-looking magazine, so what harm is there in it?* The harm may not occur at the time, but if the spark is kept lit, it will only get bigger and more dangerous. Keep this in mind when you make a mistake, repeatedly, and you keep the fire lit.

Fire is one of the best examples to use. A spark can take down an entire forest. When a house is on fire, the family loses everything. Fire affects our lives, but it can also affect our lifestyle choices. Time and time again, I hear about lives being destroyed by bad choices. I have read about powerful people living a life of luxury then dying. What did they take with them? Nothing. Not even their clothes. Then what?

I get so sad when I hear of people taking their lives, rejecting Christ. Every day we read and hear about someone taking their own life because in their minds, this life doesn't fit or need them anymore. Why not? Who made it this way? Why not stick around and make it better? People who take their lives struggle to find one good reason to not commit suicide. I know this to be true because I was tempted several times throughout my life. Each time I tried to end my life, I couldn't go through with it because I knew I would face Christ.

Tragically, too many are so burnt up with Satan's lies they wish they could change their minds but don't have the strength to do it. They make their choice with a sharp knife, a bottle of pills, or the trigger of a gun. Dying without Christ is a never-changing chance to return to this earth. Another lie from the devil. You are not better off dead!

While I still battle with temptations, I know how to deal with them now. That is, I know where to run for strength, mercy, and power to overcome those temptations. That is what God will do for you. I make mistakes, as will you, as does everyone, but I try to not give into sexual sins. Satan may tempt me, but I try to not open his door. I live one day at a time.

## Let's Get It Straight

There is a God. No matter what you believe or what you think doesn't remove the truth that God does exist. Nothing can evolve from nothing. Somebody had to be the beginning. Somebody had to create all that we see, smell, hear, touch, and taste. It can't just happen. That's impossible. So instead of using energy to try and prove that there is no God, wouldn't it be easier to ask him if he does exist? He has proven himself to multitudes. He will prove himself to you.

Many people see God in a narrow image, but he sees a big picture. Look at the plan that God has for man and then see how we ruined it. God is all-knowing. He always existed.

I used to wonder where God came from, what world he lived in. Was he so bored that he made us? I always knew and believed in God, but I had a weak, inaccurate perception of who he was. I treated him like I would another person in my life. I wanted to take advantage of his love for me. How often have you heard this? "If God really loves me, he won't hurt me" or "If God really loves me, he won't send me to hell."

It's true that God loves you, but he is a *just God* also. His character is holy. God hates what sin does to people. He does not delight in seeing people hurt, and he knows sin will and does hurt people. "The wages of sin is death" (Romans 6:23). But which one of us obeys every thing that God asks us to do?

When I became a Christian while in junior high, I never received discipleship. Nobody invested in me to teach me how to live the righteousness of God, so I tried to learn on my own who God was, who was this Jesus. I saw movies about Christ, and I believed what I saw. To this day, I still believe, but throughout my life I did not appreciate redemption and salvation. I would ask, "Why all this blood on the cross?" It would take decades for me to learn that Jesus shed his blood on the cross to save me! My wages of sin would be paid because of his perfect sacrifice, and I could be spared eternity in hell. Then I read up on hell and who goes there. I knew that I was a Christian, and God would never send me to hell. This was true, but I should have listened and obeyed God.

*OK, I will listen and try to obey, but these magazines give me lustful thoughts. So, I'm going to find out why, but only on my terms. I will believe what I want to and ignore what bothers me the most.*

Fifteen

# Counting the Cost of Pornography

I figured being a Christian would give me a ticket to sin freely. That's what many Christians are doing today. They don't count on the consequences of sin. They rest with the thought of a good God not caring about their sin because he's already paid the price. They think God will let them get away with whatever they choose. Inevitably, consequences are too great to bear, and down they go. I can't tell you how many times I was sinning just to get up and sin again. Deep down, every time I got up, I knew I was heading toward a life of failures.

As a young man, I thought I was invincible, as most young men believe. *Nothing will happen to me that I can't handle. I won't get into anything that I can't walk away from when I feel like it.*

## The Big Business of Pornography

Billions of dollars are spent on the porn industry every year. Back in the sixties, pornography was available but not as easy to get as it is today. I knew which neighbor threw away their old copies of dirty magazines and waited till it got dark on the days before trash pickup. Then, I found a hiding place for them in my home. Something always told me not to pick them up, but my desires were telling me to look at them.

*It Only Takes One Look*

Women who pose in any adult magazine have one goal, and that is to make money. They use men's natural desires to view more so they will buy more, but the life of a porn model lasts only a short time. Who's next, a prettier girl? One who shows more, that entices more?

The editorials tell you that these women are hot, that it's only natural to look at them. They tell you that the next issue will star the most beautiful young women—maybe a campus girl, maybe a housewife. Back when I was young, porn was concentrated in magazines. I will not name the magazines. They do not deserve to be recognized. This industry has destroyed many men. It has changed our culture. Homes are broken up, and the pornographic industry destroys masculinity and men's leadership. Men are arrested for viewing child pornography.

Most men will tell you that pornography is a natural part of our culture. If that is true, then they must define the kind of culture we live in. What will living in a society of self-pleasers do for a people? I believe that what goes in your mind can dictate who you become unless you get rid of it right away. Second Peter 2:19 reads, "They promise them freedom, while they themselves are slaves to depravity—for 'people are slaves to whatever has mastered them.'"

I knew pornography was ruining my life. It controlled me. The lure of women in the magazines exerted power over me. The images were so powerful that they would stay in my mind until they lost their flavor, like an old piece of gum. Then, I would quickly run to replace the old images with new, more delightful ones.

The looks intrigued me about the girls, and the stories of the girls led me to desire experiences with them, and so on as

I spiraled out of control. At first, I desired single ladies, then it became married women. Then hardcore pornography took over. I wanted more, so I found more.

Then, when I got older, I spent a lot of money on my sexual appetite. Along with the changing culture came the changing adult industry. Society looked the other way while the women became more vulgar and the guys spent more money to see vulgar ladies dance on a pole.

There is always a fall with sin. I might have kept my magazines secret from others, but my reckless, self-centered behavior was no secret. My moods were erratic. When I thought someone might catch me, I would get scared and defensive. I couldn't live without the sexual images. I wanted to find out all I could so I could act out my fantasies. That's exactly what I did, but I never thought of the consequences of what I was about to do. I never counted the cost. Tell me, who does at the time?

When the thoughts and feelings toward sexual habits become overwhelming, most of us just give in. It was easier to give in to impulses because to quit would mean I would have to admit I had a problem. I was too proud to admit I was addicted, like some weakling, I thought.

Most men, over the course of their lifetime, will have likely seen porn in one way or another. Some can see it and walk away. Some might even glance long enough to laugh about it but still they walk away. Many more won't walk away. They take one look after another until they believe it's natural to have those thoughts.

## Technology Fuels the Flame

Somewhere in our young lives, many of us are introduced

## It Only Takes One Look

to pornography, and that one look leads us down a path of unthinkable sin, irreplaceable loss, and immeasurable damage. The one who is raised on pornography, the one who keeps it, nurtures it, loves it, and acts on it is one who faces unimaginable consequences.

That was me. I grew up with it. When the internet was introduced into our homes, I was thrilled because now not only could I view it on the computer, but also I could talk to females about sexual things. I could test the waters via the computer to see what kind of girl I was speaking to.

This prevalence of porn has gone from a spark to an out-of-control fire. This epidemic has reached almost every nation on this planet via the internet. The computer was once used for proper communication, but some of us turned it into a playing field of hungry men looking for women and girls. New websites pop up every day offering views of the most wicked of pictures.

Who cares about the feelings of victims whose pictures are blasted from one site to another? Once a picture is posted on the internet, it will stay there throughout that person's lifetime and beyond. Think about that every time you view such photos. That girl has grown up, but her picture remains. She now may be forty years old, maybe married with children of her own. Think about how she feels, not how you feel. You are looking at her with the intent to please yourself. You don't have her permission, do you? Every time you view a picture, you are supporting that website in its business of ruining lives. When you pass pictures from one to another, you are making that woman's picture more available to more men.

Pornography is an addiction that rips to the soul of the offender and the victims. Children are traded and kidnapped from their parents so they may be used in adult pictures, movies, and even prostitution rings. Children grow up every day with their futures stolen from them by pornography and its effects on people and families.

Consider the innocence of a child that is stolen by pornography. With no vision for a future, that child lives at the command of the photographer, without value or personal identity. Then, when the photographer has found a new treasure cove, the "has-been" lives on the streets where a pimp picks her up. He offers her drugs, telling her they will help her feel better, perform better, forget about her doubts and fears. At first the pimp treats her nice, convincing her she can make money by using her body. Why not? Isn't that what she was doing before?

Now she is trapped into drugs and prostitution. When she doesn't perform for the pimp, she is beaten. She may try to commit suicide. Finally, she feels that her life is useless to society. The pimp got what he wanted. He knows that there are other girls out there.

Most of the time, you see these girls around adult places, trying to get customers. What's behind them? An adult bookstore. Isn't that where it all began? There is another side to this story as well. One day women who use their bodies to entice men will be accountable to God. How often do we hear the feminist response? "This is my body. I will do whatever I want with it. Nobody tells me what to do."

Contrary to what many believe, our bodies are not our own. We belong to the Creator. You never created your body, nor I mine. You were made by God. Your body does not belong to you. God may allow you to use your body the way

*It Only Takes One Look*

you choose, but that doesn't change who owns it.

Pornography plays a significant role in the destruction of our society. Some might not see the effects right away, but those who read, look, and hide their pornography affect society, in addition to their own personal lives. They affect the way people think, act, live. Most don't see the deep effect it has on families. The use of pornography broke up all my marriages. When I think about it, all my sexual activities, indiscretions, adultery, and fornication could be traced back to all those books and magazines I looked at throughout my life. I stared at the pictures and then acted out my fantasies. I knew the magazines were Satan's favorite attempts to destroy me, to get into my thoughts, to lead me into sexual sin. He replaces family values with impure thoughts that lead to cheating, and even, in many cases, to physical abuse. Divorce quickly follows.

## Who Loses?

We all lose. Pornography isn't just some innocent magazines that, like many young people believe, are a normal part of life. If porn is so great, why not have pornographic materials in the doctor's office or some other public place? Have you picked up some of the popular magazines today to see some model or a celebrity loosely or barely clothed? This is pornography too because it entices. When men see a picture of a scantily dressed woman in a magazine, they think, *Wow, nice legs! I wonder what she looks like with all her clothes off.*

Do not be fooled, ladies, into thinking that your man doesn't think or fantasize about those women. What increases a man's sexual thoughts? The less a woman wears. I may be stepping into a sensitive area for men and women, but reality proves how we are manipulated into attraction for scantily clad women.

Even advertisers know that sex sells. Thus, there are Calvin Klein ads of men in underwear and hundreds if not thousands of companies who use nearly naked women to sell their products. Next is nude pornography—the most dangerous for a man's mind. When a man's curiosity gets bored with looking at clothed women, he wants to see more. So, what's available? Magazines showing women nude. When I was young, pornography was mild compared with today's pornography. Back then, there was still a lot left to the imagination, but today you don't have to imagine anything. It's always available to view.

Why go to an adult bookstore when you can see whatever you like instantly from the comfort of your own home on the computer? What should have been stopped in the past has become the main source for men who sexually abuse women and children. Most of the time, I just happened upon the hardcore. But when I found it, it instantly produced sexual thoughts. Little has been done to rid it from our computers. Technology has led us to amazing breakthroughs in medicine, science, education, and more. Yet people continue to be more destructive to our society, and we refuse to protect our youth from these sites. Always an excuse! Years of excuses have brought us to a world of sexual predators attempting to kidnap our children.

I read in the newspaper today about a mother doing meth in her garage while her nine-year-old daughter was being assaulted. She was so high that it took two days before her daughter could tell her about the event. Two days! Then she reported it to the police. Who were these men? These men spent the night at her place, while her daughter slept. What a sad story. Who's the victim? The daughter. I bet if those men were to speak (which they won't), they would tell you that they regularly view child pornography. It's available. If nothing is done about this, the trend will continue.

I wonder if all those years of doing nothing is too late for our kids. If I could get pornography decades ago when I was a kid, don't you think it's easier for today's young people? Sexting between kids is a current trend that will continue to break the family apart. Sure, some kids get counseling, but this world's counsel will fail our youth by not getting to the heart of the problem. Any fix from this world—from schools, psychologists, or prescription drugs—is only temporary. We cannot look away from this problem. Why don't Americans stand up against the adult industry? Maybe it's because it hasn't happened to your family. But as Americans, we all are family. Shouldn't we all care?

## Pornography Destroys Marriages

Wives don't want to find out that their husbands are looking at porn. What message does that leave for her? After all, when two people get married, they tell one another, "Till death do you part." When pornography is brought into the marriage, the marriage is no longer between two people. This may be blunt, but I believe that many men fantasize about other women when they are making love to their wives. Some therapists say that this is normal (a few of mine did). Just what you would expect from a culture that is twisted?

What will you say to your children when they find your secret hiding place full of pornographic magazines? What will you say to your son when he asks you why these women are naked in the magazines? What will you say when your children ask you if Mommy knows? How will you explain to your wife the numerous women you have brought into the marriage? Do you think your neighbors will care if you get caught? Who will defend you when you knew it was wrong? How can you comfort your wife when you lose your integrity as the leader in your home?

## Progression of a Porn Marriage

1. The wife leaves you or kicks you out in the streets. Your children wonder about Daddy. Your wife ends up lying to your kids.

2. Your wife goes through emotional trauma because she doesn't understand why you would do this to your family. No matter how you try to convince her that you will change, she won't accept it.

3. You now make your wife vulnerable to some other guy.

4. Here comes your divorce. Your kids are affected. The court decides who gets the kids. You constantly fight. You threaten each other.

5. You each choose new partners. Your children grow up thinking that it's all right to get a divorce if your marriage doesn't work out. Then the cycle begins again, but this time your children are the ones affected.

When I think about my first marriage, I still can't get over what I threw away. Sue was so sweet and a great wife. She didn't deserve what I put her through. Those thoughts will never go away and the regrets still linger, but if I let them control me, I won't be of much use to the Lord.

Pornography destroys. Isn't that what the devil does? Are you willing to lose your families, guys? Next time you have your family together, ask yourself, "Is this magazine so worth it to lose what I have? Do I love my wife or this thing?" Next time your children are hugging you, ask yourself, "Do I want them to follow down the path of pornography?" Can you see your child looking at a naked person on the internet? How does that make you feel? Your children are watching you. They see the moods you have after coming home from going to watch the girls dancing naked. Could it be the guilt showing on your face?

I used to come home moody, angry, and bitter. My wife used to ask me why I was acting so strange. I would be so mean to her because the guilt made me feel like I didn't want to be around her. I didn't deserve being around her. I knew she would find out sooner or later, so I put up a front. Just because I put up a front didn't mean everything would be okay. To the contrary, my consequences affected my family drastically. What I did caused great hardship for my wife, my kids, and anyone else close to me.

My son died without me ever making it right with him. I have never seen my three grandsons. My daughters still have a hard time talking to me. They say what I've done is in the past, but I see how difficult it is for them sometimes to communicate with me. The consequences fell on my children. Of course, the best I can do now is love my children with all my heart, show them as much as they'll allow, and let the Lord speak to them.

We live in a day where our children are growing up with

little to no values at all. Domestic disturbances in the family are at an all-time high. No wonder kids grow up to think that marriage is a joke, an experiment at best! Just live with each other, they think, and if it doesn't work out then go find someone else. "No one gets hurt." Isn't that called *fornication*?

Marriage is very important to God. He ordained it. He performed the first marriage. He set standards for marriage. Just because man has found a way to change the standards doesn't mean that God has changed. He will never change his holy character to accommodate man's definition of marriage. It doesn't matter what the laws say. What will remain true and everlasting is what God says.

The man is supposed to be the head of the home. Since many men don't want to accept that responsibility, our structure in society is and will continue to collapse. Look at the latest news. Kids are joining gangs because the dads are not in the picture at home. Moms are raising sons without dads. Mothers struggle to make ends meet while fathers lie in prison or on the couch or back alley strung out on drugs. Dads are on the run without paying child support. We opened the door to accept politically correct changes.

Without the godly structure of marriage, our American values are lost, as will be our American success. We wonder why some of our kids commit suicide. They feel hopeless from as early as they can remember without models of hope in the home, or without a home at all.

## Pornography Breeds Destructive Marriages

Many of the magazines in the eighties began testing the waters more and more with "alternative" lifestyles, such as lesbian-gay lifestyles and same-sex marriages. How did society accept this as normal? It used to be that the gay lifestyle was hidden in the closet, but for some reason someone stuck their head out the door and demanded equality.

America accepts any adult lifestyle as normal, yet the Word of God clearly distinguishes between natural and unnatural, and between righteous living and abomination. People don't want to hear what God says about this.

Sometimes it bothers me to talk about it, but the truth is, all this is unacceptable to God. The gay community doesn't want to hear what the Bible says, or they misquote it, or put words in God's mouth—a very dangerous habit.

This is not about love. It's about lust. One of my favorite Bible passages deals with the condition of mankind when they turn their backs on their Creator:

> *The wrath of God is being revealed from heaven against all the godlessness and wickedness of people, who suppress the truth by their wickedness, since what may be known about God is plain to them, because God has made it plain to them. For since the creation of the world God's invisible qualities—his eternal power and divine nature—have been clearly seen, being understood from what has been made, so that people are without excuse.*
>
> *For although they knew God, they neither glorified Him as God nor gave thanks to Him, but their thinking became futile and their foolish hearts were darkened. Although they claimed to be wise, they became fools and exchanged the glory of the immortal God for images made to look like a mortal human being and birds and animals and reptiles.*

> *Therefore, God gave them over in the sinful desires of their hearts to sexual impurity for the degrading of their bodies with one another. They exchanged the truth of God for a lie and worshipped and served created things rather than the Creator—who is forever praised. Amen.*
>
> *Because of this, God gave them over to shameful lusts. Even their women exchanged natural relations for unnatural ones. In the same way the men also abandon natural relations with women and were inflamed with lust for one another. Men committed shameful acts with other men and received in themselves the due penalty for their error.*
>
> *Furthermore, just as they did not think it worthwhile to retain the knowledge of God, he gave them over to a depraved mind, so that they do what ought not to be done. They have become filled with every kind of wickedness, evil, greed and depravity. They are full of envy, murder, strife, deceit and malice. They are gossips, slanders, God-haters, insolent, arrogant and boastful; they invent ways of doing evil; they disobey their parents; they have no understanding, no fidelity, no love, no mercy. Although they know God's righteous decree that those who do such things deserve death, they not only continue to do these very things but also approve of those who practice them* (Romans 1:18–32).

This passage is as true today as it was when it was written to the Christian churches in Rome. The Bible talks a lot about immorality. If you look at this last verse, you will read that those who approve are also deserving the same punishment.

So, do you accept this lifestyle as normal, or is God a liar? Just because the law says that I must accept the gay lifestyle as normal doesn't mean that I must. If I get into trouble because I oppose this ungodly act of living, my conscience will be at rest knowing I abide by the truth of the Lord.

God created man and woman. He told them to marry one another. What else is there to say? Does man have the right to change God? How much longer will it take for us to stop making up our own way of living? Just because laws are passed allowing you to get married to anyone doesn't mean that you're married in God's eyes.

When God ordained the marriage of Adam and Eve, the institution began as it was intended. Creating a man-made law to attempt to change God's law only brings hardship upon this country. We don't, as a nation, have the right to determine how we want to live when the standards of living are set forth by God.

I learned about homosexuals through magazines. I saw lesbian pictures, but I never expected the lifestyle to go as far as it has today. We should always strive to love people, no matter their lifestyles, but never compromise on their choice of lifestyles because they are choosing to live in sin. My speaking against the lifestyle does not mean I hate those that fall into this sin, either willingly or due to the addictions formed from their childhoods.

Most everything God creates and ordains, Satan will offer a counterfeit for it. Marriage is honorable before God between a man and a woman. Outside of God's desire, a marriage between two men or two women is counterfeit, evil. We are going down a dangerous road.

If I say that I disagree with the gay lifestyle, the world considers me a hateful person. If I oppose them by speaking out against the lifestyle, I am "unfair" and "intolerable" to what the world sees as a lovely ceremonial marriage. Yet, I live by the truth of my Creator.

Throughout the Bible are warnings and examples of people and nations that chose to live by their lustful desires rather than by the truth of God.

Wouldn't it be simpler to obey God than to challenge his authority and face the consequences? Our behavior is tearing apart this nation. It is tearing apart the minds of our youth. God will not continue allowing us to accept this lust for one another. There are consequences. Can't you see it happening right in front of your eyes? Why do you think our government is in disarray? They pass laws allowing same-sex couples to live together as man and wife, while one pretends to be the other. Who gives this approval? Is it the government? Is it the people? Do you approve of yourself making up these rules?

You are being lied to. You are being deceived. Yet, the final choice is yours. As always, it's about lust. Satan is telling you that it's love because you have feelings for him or her. You can't depend upon feelings because they are deceiving.

I lusted after my three wives. I never loved them. I wasted forty-four years driven by lust, not love. And lust is all about the person with the lust, where love is about the person being loved.

To illustrate how bad this world has become, I talked with five guys in a van last week. I was sitting up front, so I tried to have a dialogue with the van driver. He laughed and scoffed at the fact I was writing a book about the effects of pornography. What God had done in my life, this man was mocking, denying. Then he made a strange comment that took me by surprise. He said, "After God made Adam and Eve, he blew it. God walked away. We are left to fend for ourselves. God is not in control. The government is in control. God didn't make me. My mother did. I don't control how people live, and neither should anybody else. Immorality is what you make of it."

Every time I tried to inject the truth, he just kept attacking God. I had to remember that Jesus went through the same thing. People laughed at and denied him. As I listened to this driver spew his misunderstandings and lies, I was struck by how far away people have turned against the God who loves them. It was hard for me to not take the man's insults personally. For me, when people mock my Lord, I am included. I know who was behind this. I know that the Lord has won the war against evil, but all Christians remain on the battlefield until he comes again.

The guys in the van admitted they loved to look at lesbian pornography. They talked about it like it was natural. Is this what you want your children to hear? No matter how people try to twist the truth, it can never change. What an honor to stand up for Christ. What an honor to be persecuted because of Jesus' name.

I learned a lot that day. This is an uphill climb. We must stand firm and speak out against unbiblical lifestyles, which will ultimately reach kids. As if this country doesn't have enough major problems, these small groups of people come up with the transgender agenda. Are we supposed to support the right to change your gender because you think God made a mistake? Now they want to have the rights to go into any restroom. This doesn't just open the door; it flies the doors off the hinges so sexual crimes can run rampant right in front of the superstore. Sex offenders getting into stadium restrooms, men stalking women posing as a transgender—these are what society is agreeing to when it supports the transgender agenda.

On the news yesterday, I saw high schools complaining about transgender men winning races in women's sports events. *Why are you complaining?* I wonder. *Isn't that what you wanted?*

Don't expect the evangelical Christians to support this. We won't, because we can't. You can try to change your physical features, but in God's eyes, you are what he made you to be. When you stand before him, you will be the gender you were born to be.

Our government is allowing these small groups to change the morals that built this country. Many people vote in support of these small, anti-Christian groups. I know many gay people, and while I get along well with them, I also know they live hopeless, lonely lives. Nevertheless, I won't turn my back on them. God doesn't. He loves them. He always has. It's sin and disobedience he hates.

## Pornography and Prostitution Together

Prostitution goes way back to the Old Testament. In Genesis 38, the story of Judah and Tamar reveals sin in God's people. Tamar was a widow, and Judah was her father-in-law. One day she dressed up as a shrine prostitute. She covered her face so Judah wouldn't recognize her.

Judah offered her goats for payment, but he would send them to her later, leaving her instead with a pledge—his seal, cord, and staff. He slept with her, and she became pregnant.

After Judah left, she changed back into her widow clothes, but when Judah found out she was pregnant, he had her brought to him to be burned alive. Before she was to be executed, she showed him three items he had left with her after their shared sin.

Judah recognized they were his and told her she was more righteous than him. He must have felt like a fool. What was culturally accepted was not pleasing to God, yet God's grace was evident through even this horrid situation. God still condemns prostitution.

I can remember while being stationed in Germany that I paid a prostitute. Back then it was cheap. Along with my porn magazines, I also desired to be with more women. The thrill of being with other women didn't come without big difficulties in my life. When I hired prostitutes, most of the time it was while being married. I listened to the wrong guys in the barracks. My choices seemed innocent at first, until the more I went to the chapel, the more convicted I felt. I had fun with the people in church and had fun with the guys in the barracks. The more I learned about God, the easier it was to walk away from these women. I take no delight in what I did, but I rejoice in God's loving grace.

Prostitution now includes young children being trafficked into sex slaves. Innocent children are being taken from their parents and their bodies sold to make money for a pimp. They have no choice or they get beaten. Pictures and videos are taken of them, then put on the computer for anyone to view.

## Counting the Cost of Pornography

I heard that one of every three children from the ages of eleven to fourteen have had nudity sent to their phones. In high school there's sexting. Many local governments fear to pass harsh laws to stop it. Many parents are shocked when they find out that their daughter has been sexting and some guy has just posted her picture on the internet. So here we go again, pictures of children are traded all over the web.

I wouldn't know what it feels like to be a prostitute, but I know by talking to them that they believe this is quick money. "Just as long as my pimp takes care of me," they say. When they get too old to trick, then what? Some become homeless or give up living in a revolving door that seems to never stop. Who are the number-one customers? Men. Who are most of the pimps? Men. Instead of protecting our women like God told us to, we use them. Some abuse their wives and children. Women are not safe walking our streets alone for fear they may be kidnapped and sold. I was shocked to hear that this is happening in America.

Just as there was hope for me leaving decades of pornography, there is hope for women who are involved in this lifestyle too. I know it is hard to get out, and it's hard living in fear of a pimp who can abuse, torture, or even kill you. The men who do this will be accountable one day before God. As fast as the police clear the streets, the women advertise on websites and porn sites.

I can remember numerous times driving in circles just to get the women's attention. I loved to see them on the streets. While I was driving around, my thoughts kept going back and forth. I knew defiling myself with a prostitute was wrong and I knew I was being tempted, but the longer I drove around looking at those women, the more my mind was telling my body I wanted to be with one of them. I kept asking the ladies how much, but I would continue driving for hours. Then I gave in to the temptation.

Every single time when I left a prostitute, I felt so sick inside. I had given money to some pimp who was using this woman to further this lifestyle. I knew that God was watching what I was doing. I felt embarrassed, because I knew it was wrong before I gave in. The power that sexual desire has over men, as I have confessed, can be devastating and unbearable.

A prostitute is a quick way to get release from the desire, even if it's only until the next time. But I had no excuse. My wife was at home. Many times, I couldn't go home right away. When I did go home, I quickly took a shower. I might have cleaned my body, but I still had a dirty mind. I grew up in filth and never relinquished it to God.

I kept my desires hidden, but I knew they were no secret to God. In every marriage I cheated on my wife with prostitutes. Did my wives know? Absolutely not, but I guess they will know now. So, I added this to my list of failures. One by one I kept sinking lower. I always fought in my mind to not give in, but I had the urge to be with someone else other than my wife.

I pray that you are getting the big picture of what immorality becomes. These behaviors destroy how people view Christian values. Then you start to question God in all of this. How can God allow innocent children and women to be used like this? Since God is in total control, it is amazing how he uses the worst situations to change lives.

## Pornography in Hollywood, and Social Media

Some of us get tired of hearing opinions from entertainers on the award shows, talk shows, and at concerts. Usually what they have to say makes little sense, if any at all. Much too often the social media covers their comments, and the public will buy into it. If you disagree with what they believe is right, they will speak out in public against you.

I don't know why we listen to them. Their job is to put on an act, something that isn't real, most of the time. Their lives are a fantasy, so why interview them? Why do so many people applaud a gay woman who has a talk show? Could it be she acts just like the rest of us? She is funny and has a great since of humor. But does that make two women living together right?

Does Hollywood think that God will change his mind, because they say so, or do they think of God at all? Most Hollywood people don't believe in our Lord and Savior Jesus Christ. They believe in science or a god that will favor their beliefs.

All my life I have read and heard about Hollywood people being depressed, doing hard prescription drugs, drinking to death, transferring spouses from one to another through divorces. They act lewd in front of cameras, accepting awards with political comments, dressing perverted while dancers on stage grab themselves. They want you to think that this is a normal way of life. They get rich, go to exclusive parties, and get interviewed on talk shows slamming Christians for our belief in morals. They get rich because we watch them act, and, then again, we love to read about their failures as well.

The business of the paparazzi reveals secrets of adultery,

## It Only Takes One Look

fornication, drugs, backstabbing, and so on. We enjoy reading about some of their pathetic lives, lives full of depression. The media reports on every move of some famous person who has gone down the wrong road. We can't check out at the cashier without reading about some weight loss program that some star is using, only to read a few months or years later that the same star is in an exclusive rehab center trying to overcome a serious drug addiction for the third or fourth time.

Then there is the television. At the click of a button, 250 channels are instantly available. Watch porn anytime. Primetime television has even changed in the past five years. I saw a program where two men were using sexual gestures with each other. I have seen men kissing each other on TV. I never thought I would ever see this on primetime TV. Hollywood keeps testing the audience to see what they can get by with. If the audience approves, then they just go up another step. They say sex sells. It's all about the money. The music industry falls in the same disgusting patterns as well.

I used to listen to songs about love when I was younger, then one by one the songs went from love to sex. Now songs glorify lusting after one another. Many lyrics tell the listener what they want to hear—about sex and more sex, disrespect for life and for authority, how bad parents are, or how bad an individual is if he or she doesn't agree with the mainstream. They make fun of female body parts, mothers, and women in general. I recall one song (likely there are many) about a couple who was having an affair while they were married to another. They had to keep this love affair a secret because that didn't want to break up their "happy" home. The song described how they couldn't help themselves because they were in love with each other. The entire song, even the chorus, openly labeled themselves as adulterers, and it was a Billboard hit! Sure, the instrumentation and the melody were pleasing to the ear. Even their voices and harmony were beautiful, but the lyrics! The music was great, but the words encouraged cheating on your spouse. Why break up your happy home if it's so happy? So, you stress out every day so you can be together, why? Because you're in love? Then the same group came out with another song about being in love, raising a family, and staying together always. Hold on a second, which way is it? Many songwriters contradict themselves.

One song may sing of true love to one "destined" person, while the next big hit by the same group sings of how to do whatever (and whomever) makes you feel good at the time, implying to ignore the consequences of infidelity. Music is a war with words. Music is so powerful that it can change some people to live their lives following the words they hear in a song. Then we see musicians singing on stage, barely clothed. Some rock bands scare the pants off us normal people. The members dress evil, look evil, and scream like they belong in an insane asylum, but some young people like this.

I saw a motorcyclist parking his bike one day. I heard yelling that was louder than his bike. When he turned his bike off, oh my, the screaming was scary. Then out from the apartment ran this two-year-old boy into his father's arms. That was so sweet, but I wondered if that little boy would eventually look and act like his father.

It seems to me that Hollywood loves to stretch the truth just to keep rich, but sooner or later life ends, and the wealth stays on earth. Is it worth it then to get your afternoon delight, then pray to your god who you think rewards your behavior.

I have learned over the years not to adapt my life according to what others say. Rather, I know now I need to keep my life according to God's plan on how to live. We all are sinners, but we all can be saved by God's grace, if we will accept his truth and love.

When I think of Hollywood and media, I think of sex, drugs, violence, and immorality that it has come to represent today. Why has society become so willing, even hungry, for such content? It has become a normal part of life. Even the news displays horrid images of violence, sexual immorality, and drug-related scenes. It's part of our culture.

What it really means is that we have become agreeable with the things of evil and are disobeying more and more of God's direction. Of course, when society feels the weight of a crisis, such as 9/11 or the Sandy Hook massacre, a loud cry to God for help fills the news headlines, social media, and radio spots.

We know, deep down inside, where to go in times of trouble, but if Christians don't take the time to know their heavenly Father, then how can they expect God to listen and respond back? To know about him is not the same as knowing him personally.

We might not say it out loud, but we only acknowledge God when we're desperate. Otherwise, we live however we want to live, regardless of what God says. Your lifestyle does affect our country. Most of the time, lives are being torn apart. How many lives will it take before God gets our attention?

The truth is, we do need God. These lifestyles I have

mentioned are tearing us, as a people, a society, and a country, apart.

## Pornography Results in Murder

Abortion is often the result of someone who either committed fornication or adultery. While there are other circumstances that people point to as reasons why they abort, the subject is a hot topic today. Either you are for saving the lives of babies or for killing them. The truth about abortion is this: God gives life, and he takes life. When you kill your baby, you will be held accountable for that decision. It really doesn't matter what you think about a fetus, whether it's a child or not. The truth is that since Adam and Eve, the process of having a child is the same. It still takes a man and a woman to have a child. The sperm gives life to a small cell. When conceived, they produce a living baby. When you murder your child, you break up that process, which is called life.

Still, God is in control even when you take your child's life. He may allow you to abort your child, but you still will be held accountable for rejecting this gift from God. A child! Life is supposed to be celebrated as if God were handing you a baby in your arms. He wants you to raise it to glorify his name. He wants you to teach your child the values from God.

Why all the abortions? Why do you want to kill your baby? When did this happen? Once again, we go back to lust that resulted in sex, which produced your child. It wasn't the child's fault that you chose to perform a sinful act. It takes sex to have a child. Most of the time it's fornication.

You are lied to from those who disrespect you and your child, those who play God. They hand you propaganda saying that this child could affect your future. Maybe you can't afford one, or you're too young. "Who will feed this child? Who will raise them?" After you have the abortion, it's too late. You can't go back and reverse it. Since the baby is a life, can we say that you murdered your child? Yet, the federal government passes laws allowing women to have abortions. Our government shares in the responsibility for every child's blood that has been shed.

No one has the right to take another person's life. A baby is a person. You can't twist the truth on abortion. Early- or late-term abortion is still killing an innocent child. Stop having unprotected sex, or stop the act altogether. I consider abortion as one of the factors why America may be getting closer to God's judgment.

From the time of conception, that child was given a soul, just like the mother was. You may kill the body, but you can't kill the soul. The doctor may rip out the body of the innocent child, but he can't rip out the soul. So, when the baby dies, it goes into the arms of Christ. That child arrives in heaven.

Like all sin, God will forgive you if you repent. He will remove the guilt of your child's death. When you receive Christ, you receive hope to one day see your aborted child in heaven. How much longer will we keep testing God's patience? Taking a child's life because you made a mistake is irresponsible. Wouldn't it be smarter to give your child up for adoption, or be responsible and raise your child? When you decide to abort your child, you alone will be at fault. Why make a baby suffer in such a way?

Satan has always hated God's creation. He loves to take lives, no matter how he does it. If he can convince you with lies to have an abortion, and you do it, that's one human taken from this earth. He thought that if he could keep me trapped into pornography that I would turn away from God, but I never denied my faith in Christ. I had a fight on my hands, but now I have the chance to tell you how wicked his lies are.

I believe that abortion is often the result of sexual sin rooted in lust, not love. America politicians keep telling us that it should be the woman's right. That's kind of true. The woman makes the choice, but if she is continuously being told that the child is a nuisance, that the child is not a person until it's born, then she is being manipulated into an abortion.

Planned Parenthood is nothing but a butcher shop with no respect for the human body or life, selling body parts, tearing apart a baby as if it were a chicken. Every doctor that performs this surgery will one day stand before God and be judged for every life they took. One day they will have a chance to think about all those babies they killed, but it won't be in heaven, unless they repent now and stop these murders. Why doesn't Planned Parenthood show the mother the fetus after the doctor kills it? Of course, they won't. When I think of babies being murdered, it fuels my hate toward the devil. I often wonder what those babies would have become. We will never know.

Mothers face difficult depression due to the guilt of abortion, yet they are not told to expect this. Instead, the decision to kill a child is presented as the key to returning to normal life and a promise of a better future, without the burden of a kid. After the abortion, many walk out feeling lonely. An hour ago, you had something that was a part of you, but now you have time to *feel* the weight of your decision. "Mommy, why did you throw me away like trash? Didn't you ever love me?" Like so many other choices in life, abortion wreaks havoc on a society. Pornography and abortion are linked by the immorality both represent.

Sixteen

# The World in Need of Hope

I have told you the "whats" and the "hows" of my life, but I want to explain the hardest for me to understand, which is the "why." Even still today, I ask God, "Why?"

Only after God told me to read the whole Bible did I finally see some of the big picture of his plan. Starting from man's fall, to a stubborn people, to Christ's death, burial, and resurrection, I now understand why the Lord is calling his people to repent.

After rededicating my life to the Lord, I have no more shame. Why not? Because when I came to understand the grace and mercy of the Lord, I knew that when I repented of all my sins, he took them all away. I knew that I was saved, but I also knew that I needed to give him my will in order to live free from what had held me hostage for forty-four years. During those years, I gave God bits and pieces of my life but never submitted my sexual habits. God wanted it all. Not parts. He knows that holding on to small sin will keep producing the same ones repeatedly.

Remember when I told you that my friends think that God has left us? I know that the Lord was always with me. No matter how wicked I lived and the lives I hurt, he was always with me. Even when I talked back to him, he was there. When I was with the prostitutes, he was there. He was with the baby that I paid to be aborted. All the times I fell on my knees over the guilt of what I had done, he was there to pick me up. Even though he knew I would return to commit the same sin repeatedly, he was there. So often we think that the Lord is stuck in one place, but it is the Holy Spirit that never leaves us nor forsakes us. If you don't know Christ, you don't have the Holy Spirit.

I didn't understand then what God was doing in my life. I didn't know from day to day that I would get worse. I truly didn't know that despite all these mistakes that I made, I would hold in my heart the truth of the Gospel. I didn't know back then that what was hidden in my heart would be more powerful than any sin I had committed. I just wanted to sin.

God never gave me a script of my life ahead of time. He just wanted me to trust in him, not listen to the devil and give in to temptation. But God was never shocked about all that I did. God is all-knowing. He knew before he made me what kind of life I would live.

I can remember the Lord asking me if I thought getting remarried the second, third, and fourth times would be any better than the first time. I smarted off by saying yes, but they never were better. I wanted to prove to God that he was wrong. My proud attitude thought I was smarter than God. As our technology advances, God's creation thinks that they have no use of him. They get their answers from a cell phone or some website, but God could cause all of those to cease to work. Then will he get your attention?

Those years of my life are done and gone. I can't go back. I wish I could. I don't know the outcome of those I have hurt, so I choose to remember the good times I had with my first wife and my children. There were many good times. I keep them in my heart. The one thing that the Lord wanted me to admit was that I knew that the actions I was deliberately committing every day were being viewed by him. He wasn't happy about me wandering off like a lost sheep. He wasn't happy about me hurting other people. My life could have been different if I would have placed my trust in him when it got tough, instead of giving up. I always was given the opportunity to walk alongside of Christ, but I let go of his hand and wandered off.

He always came after me and brought me back. Time after time I wandered off. It's not about how I was in the past; rather, it's how I am now. My hands are always holding on to his hands. I have this fear that if I let go, I will go back. So, I hold on tight. I let God take care of my past.

I can look back and see all my failures, but still I hold onto Christ. Why didn't I do that in the past? Because I acted like a child wandering away from his father, doing what he wanted, not knowing how much it would hurt Father and son.

I pouted with God. I did what a child would do. I grew up slower than my Christian brothers and sisters at the time I was saved. But my heavenly Father never turned his back nor abused me. He let the consequences fit the disobedience.

Can you see your tomorrow? Do you know the time of your death? Of course you can't and don't, but God does. We all roam around in this vast picture of God's plan. Most of the time we hardly consider the main question, "Will you be in God's final picture?"

It is your call. God is not a bully. He will not force you to accept his plan for you. You either accept Christ or you reject him and find out what happens when you do. I thank God that he allowed me to live through all those years. He could have called me home, then I would have had to face him for the life I was living, without turning my life around.

He is such a merciful God. I did test his patience, but he knew my heart better than I did, and he never lost sight of his plan for me. We make the final decision. Christ sends an invitation for us to live with him.

I even used that to sin. I knew where I was heading. How many of my brothers and sisters in Christ are doing the same thing? You might not see it because Satan has blinded your eyes and ears to the truth. Look around and see the direction your life is heading.

Are there any answers for this mess that we are living in? Does the government have the answers? Does religion have the answers? Do therapists have answers? Of course not! Most therapists use techniques that offer temporary solutions, but they never solve the real problem. Their solutions offer no peace, no contentment, no forgiveness, nor eternal hope.

## Governments and Politicians

It seems to me that repeatedly our government tries to change laws or make up new ones to please the people who voted for them. There are two parties fighting for control of our country—liberals and conservatives. In general, liberals are for abortions, same-sex marriage, and any religion you want to bring into our country. Conservatives are for the life of an unborn child from conception, marriage between one man and one woman, and a nation founded by Christian men. Although we have the freedom to worship whomever, no outside religion should have the right to take over our nation.

The battle has been between these two parties since I can remember. Many of our politicians have lost the true vision for America. Their view is dependent upon the lifestyle

## The World in Need of Hope

America people have chosen to live. The government has never had the answers to immorality because many people in the government are living in sexual sin themselves. The American people have turned their backs on the values given by God.

A people with a corrupt government will take down their nation. God will not tolerate America much longer, which once had values according to Christian principles from God's holy Word, and then turned from their God. Even some Christian churches have turned their backs on God, gone astray, becoming "lukewarm." They often preach, "As long as it doesn't affect me, then why worry about those other lifestyles? They can do whatever they want. I don't have the right to tell them how to live."

If you support any lifestyle that God has forbidden, then you're just as guilty. I wish somebody would have come along and told me how bad I was living, but I kept my sins so hidden. In my heart I knew viewing pornography was wrong, but in my mind, I accepted this as normal. So, I just did it. It's very dangerous for a Christian to disobey God, knowing that what they're doing is wrong. The presidents we have had in the last fifty years have:

- Had affairs
- Signed off on gay rights, abortion rights
- Signed treaties with enemy nations
- Sold weapons to our enemies
- Lied, then smiled at the camera
- Accepted local laws taking God out of schools and government buildings, replacing them with

religions that are against our Christian values and morals

We allow them to infiltrate our nation with their loudspeakers and buildings, and we worship their god, who is dead.

Our nation is a nation of many different cultures, but that doesn't mean we give up Christ. It is in Christ that this nation was founded. Not by Allah or Muhammed, or by any other dead man with a dead message that denies the deity of Christ. No wonder this nation is so lost! We took Christ out of the picture.

But no matter how evil our government gets, God is still in control. God knows that man is separated from him by sin, and the only way to get back that fellowship is through Christ. Name one man who ever died for a world then came back alive and was witnessed by five hundred people. Please, c'mon, tell me. Name one. You can't, because there is none. The Lord says,

*Salvation is found in no one else, for there is no other name under heaven given to mankind by which we must be saved* (Acts 4:12).

So, ask yourself this question: Is our government living its former motto, "In God We Trust?" This nation is living by two ways: "In the government" we trust or by the "people" we trust. God says we cannot serve two masters. The government has failed the people, and the people have failed themselves by trusting in material things instead of trusting in the one who created them. We American people have failed God and this country. We are a whining, stubborn country.

If you tell a woman that she looks beautiful, you could

## The World in Need of Hope

end up losing your job. If you complain about the large letters on the weather alert system because they scare people, they make the letters bigger. If you don't like the bananas in the store, tell the media how bad they are, then the store will remove them. You think I'm kidding? This is our new America.

"How dare you speak about Christ? Maybe some people don't want to hear about your God, so keep your mouth shut about him. He really doesn't exist. It's just in your mind." This is the type of conversation that governs our society today. How many times have you heard that? Then, to make it worse, somebody complains about a cross or prayer in schools or the Ten Commandments posted in a courthouse, and, boom, the elements of our nation's foundations are removed from our nation.

Are you getting the picture? We are replacing Christ with our own values, our own decisions. If something goes wrong, we will blame it on someone else. God is viewed as some old man with a staff, and his son Jesus is a wet puppy. We have had it so good that we have become complacent. No need for God to interfere unless we ask him to. Then he will do as we tell him to.

Well, my friend, I believe that God's patience is running out. America is heading toward the dead end. We are almost there. If you think that we won't face judgment because of our sinful ways, you are fooling yourself. God will not continue much more with his patience for our nation.

I believe God made America for two reasons: to support and help protect Israel from their enemies and to spread the news of salvation through Christ to the rest of the world. America has failed in both ways. We have allowed the enemies surrounding Israel to arm up against them. Of course, prophecy plays the final role, but America is still accountable. We as a Christian nation are supposed to set the standards for the rest of the world, but we have failed.

We have allowed immorality to take over our lives. So, does religion have the answers? Christianity is not the same as *religion*. Religion is some man-made beliefs that stand on the word of men who have no true basis for the condition of people. Christianity comes from a relationship with God through Jesus Christ. God has never had a beginning or an end. He created man with free will, and through man's free will, he has trusted in himself, rather than in God. Though people come up with different views of God, he is still the same.

Religion says that God will let you into heaven if you believe in whatever that *religion* decrees or says to believe in. But these religious leaders are dead in the ground. They have no value to the living. They can't take away your sins. They can't speak on behalf of God. Only Christ can. What use are they? Some say that not all Muslims are radical. If you agree with and live by the Koran, then you are radical. If you do not agree with or live by the Koran, then how can you call yourself a Muslim? If you do agree with what's written by Muhammad, then you want to annihilate Christians off the face of the earth, along with the Jews. If you disagree with Muhammad, then you are to die.

You can't have it both ways. I wonder if Mr. Muhammad would like to come back and change his teachings. His religion has answers, all right, but their answer is to rid the world of Americans. You cannot be a Muslim if you disagree with the religion's text or instruction manual, the Koran.

Then there are the American religious men from the past

that still fool many people. What can a dead man do to help you? Can he feed you? Can you have a relationship with him? Does he invite you into his home? I hope not! Can he love you? He can do nothing from the grave. But still many will believe in their teachings all they way to their graves. Then they find out the religious leader they put their trust in has lied to them. Too late! You made your decision to follow the teachings of a liar. There's no other way to put it. Some religions say that they believe in Christ. They believe that he died on the cross and rose again. They agree that no mere man could have pulled that off, yet their *religion* does not live according to his word. I want you to think about this:

1. If you believe in this, then why do you knock on doors, hoping that God will recognize that you are spreading the word of this religious leader, circumventing Christ, who is the only way to God?

2. You say that you believe that Christ died on the cross, but not for all sins, just the big ones. In God's view, sin is sin, and God hates all sin. So which ones did he leave out? If you list the big ones, then Jesus is a liar because his sole purpose was to draw all men through him to God. The smallest of sins will keep you from heaven. That's why Christ died on the cross. We don't remember every sin we do every day or what we have done in the past. But God knows.

3. Some say that Jesus was the brother of Satan, that God created both. God gave Satan the earth, and Christ heaven. If Christ only controls heaven, then how do we get past Satan to get there? No one could because the devil would own the earth, and when you die, there would be no cleansing of sin. That would mean that all humans would be lost.

4. Some say that God has so much love that he would never send anyone to hell, there are different ways to get to heaven, and we will all meet there. Some believe that you can ask another man to forgive you because he has special favor with God. But that's not true.

Why is Christianity as God has shown us in his Word so hard to accept? All over the world, Satan has put in the minds of some men to doubt what God says. Most will contradict God's Word to invent some new doctrine, which is no more than something to impress God by doing deeds and works. But that's not what God is looking for.

I compare these men to a tree. I can face it, speak to it, and tell it how much I love it, but I will get no response. It will wither away and be of no use to me. Still, more and more people are searching for an answer. We live in a dangerous world with no guarantees for tomorrow, no hope, and we wonder why drug and alcohol use are at an all-time high. People are left to believe in a creation, not the Creator.

How often have we heard, "I believe in God just as you do?" If you believed in my God, then you would believe in what he says about you and the only way to be saved. It is true! Religion has no answers. They are part of the problem—a dead message.

## Mental Health

Many therapists will give you a temporary solution, such as medication for depression, or the "let's talk it out" routine. "You should try some yoga, or let me hypnotize you." "Change your habit this way a little but remain sane." "It's what you eat, your fat intake." "It's his or her fault." "It's the

## The World in Need of Hope

culture we live in." "Take up some hobby." Some of these may produce positive results, such as a hobby or going to church and meeting new friends, but all these are still temporary. There's got to be another answer, one that brings peace now and eternal life. I can remember all the suggestions given to me to try out. I knew what I wanted, but I wasn't ready to give up my lifestyle.

I used to let the gurus tell me what the answers were, but I knew what the real answer was. Many times, I got frustrated with myself for letting them try to force their workbook on me.

If you're a believer in Christ and need therapy, you must find a strong Christian therapist, someone who uses wise Christian principles, someone who uses the Bible as corrections to sinful behaviors, someone who is loving, caring, and firm but committed to the Lord.

Americans have lost their hearts, so some therapists are making money from your bad decisions, especially from sex offenders. From the time I picked up that first pornographic magazine as a child, I carried a heavy burden of guilt for forty-four years. I used those magazines as if they were my god. They were good for taking care of my sex drive. They were good when I was bored. This was my therapy. It cost me dearly. Sin is never free. It costs. But are there answers for immorality? Are there answers for sexual criminals or sex offenders? Is there hope?

# Seventeen

# Conclusion

After forty-four years of living in sexual sin, I came to the following conclusions:

1. I was the cause of my own undoing because I knew the truth but was not willing to submit to it. I could never blame God. My wives weren't to blame. My father wasn't to blame. It wasn't even Satan. I made the decision to give in to his temptation. He tempted me with unbelievable attacks, but I didn't have to give in.

Help was always available from God. But the pleasure of sin kept me controlled. We live in a world that has replaced our minds with impure thoughts. We get help by the culture we live in, but each person must decide how they are going to live.

I decided how I wanted to live, but only God knew the outcome. I knew he was trying to get my attention. I had to take the full responsibility of all my sins. I owned what I did, but I needed to give up that ownership.

2. I determined that what I had been doing was evil, and God would not tolerate it. I thought, *How much more will it take for God to stop this?* One weekend I sat down and went over my life in my mind. I was disgusted with myself. I wanted God to let me go back and start over.

## Conclusion

3. Just to erase these painful thoughts, I thought about all the people I had hurt. I found myself on my knees calling out to God. My life was a disgrace. Throughout all those years, my heart was hurting. But I did as my mind desired, not what my heart was telling me.

4. While kneeling, I kept crying over my sins. I had always known that I was sinning against Christ who died for me. I knelt with no excuse for my behavior. I knew that Christ forgave me, but I felt like I didn't deserve to be forgiven because of the wickedness of my behavior.

5. A holy presence came over me. I knew what it was. It was the hand of the Lord on my shoulder reminding me that my sins had always been forgiven, but continuing to live in those sins was a mockery to what he did on the cross. It was knowing who I am in Christ before God that finally convicted me. God sees me perfect through Christ, but I made a mockery of the cross by using it to sin.

6. For the first time in my life I envisioned Jesus Christ as my heavenly Father. Here I was on my knees in front of my loving Father, who was correcting me. I finally was still before the Lord. I couldn't get up. I had to give up my habits and behavior. After this conviction of guilt, I felt this loving hand reaching out for me to grab onto. He wanted to hold my hand. He knew I would continue in my sexual sins unless he took control of my life. I kept still, sobbing in my state of conviction. I had lived most of my life in the darkness of human sexual desires. I was without excuse because as a Christian, I knew that my life was not Christlike.

7. I knelt there for a while, scared, because I thought that

I couldn't live without that filthy lifestyle. Of course, it was true. I couldn't change my life on my own. But the battle of giving up this lifestyle was powerful.

The thought of Christ knocking at my heart made me cry even harder. I was being broken. Then it came. I cried out for him to remove my burden. I couldn't stand the guilt of my sins. Most of all, I couldn't stand to know that Christ was watching me sin against him. I knew how he suffered to take away ALL my sins.

8. He truly is my Father, because he acted like one while I knelt before him. He never gave up on me, but instead he welcomed me back home. I gave up this evil life. Now that those sexual sins are behind me, how do I handle temptations? How do I handle being tested?

Since Christ took my hands and lifted me up off my knees, I have not let go. I live in fear of what will happen if I ever let go of his hands. That fear is a good one. I have committed my life to him. I have committed to fighting against pornography. I stand before God with his Son Jesus Christ. The powerful blood of Christ redeemed me.

After my commitment to the Lord, I have been tempted to go back to my old ways, but I won't. All I do is remember the cost of sinning. I was reminded that it takes time to heal. Through this healing process, I would be tested, but I would gain strength every time.

Never give up. Always look to Christ.

I asked God to send someone to stand with me against immorality. Sometimes I felt like I was all alone to fight against sexual sins, but I wasn't. The Holy Spirit has always been there.

## Conclusion

Are there answers? Yes! But America is going in the wrong direction. Satan is deceiving many to believe that what is sin is just normal behavior. Most think that God will understand because he is the God of love. The world answers, "It's OK to love someone of the same sex. It's OK to cheat on your wife because you don't love her anymore. It's OK to lust after other women." We act according to our feelings rather than truth. Then we take the truth and twist it to conform to our desires. Truth will never be absent from God. He is the beginning of truth. He IS TRUTH.

People cry out for help when things go bad, but to whom do they cry out? When I cried out and gave my burdens to the Lord, I never looked back. I can discuss my past with people, but I won't dwell on my past. There is nothing I can do to change it.

Since that time, the Holy Spirit keeps testing me, helping me be more obedient to my heavenly Father, which is the best way to go. I have a close relationship with the Lord. I talk with him all the time. I take everything to him. I ask him direction on what to do. I ask him what he wants me to do to serve him.

Does that mean that every time God talks to me it will be positive? What I am saying is that there will be valleys to walk through. I have been through more valleys than mountaintops. But the valleys were a place to be tested. They were the places for me to learn how to trust in the Lord. Only God can help you out of a valley. You can't climb out on your own. You keep slipping back down, and each time you slip down, the valley gets deeper. One way I serve him is by telling my story of a life that was full of sin, only to allow the power of God to transform and rescue my life from the sin of immorality. I have tried the most indecent of sexual sins.

Many believers who believe in Christ need to be transformed, but will it take a hard knee on the ground? People like me, like you, who have experienced pornography will have to surrender things like magazines, behaviors, and attitudes in favor of the Bible.

I began my story by telling you about a young boy who picked up a magazine and began to live the life these magazines were presenting as normal. But normal it wasn't. Once you turn the pages of these magazines, you're open to a world of sex and pleasure. The pleasure expands throughout this world, and the magazines approve of it. The consequences of having those magazines and pictures on our computers is deadly.

God never intended for us to live like this. God's creation is crying out for help, for hope. There is an answer to our country, but we must recognize that we have this problem and be willing to recognize our only source for help is from Christ.

There is no other way. Americans need to get on their knees before God and reject pornography in its many forms—magazines, television, movies, music, billboards, and so on. Unless and until we do, America will continue to fall. Are we willing to pay the consequences for such a vulgar society?

I'm here to tell you that we must repent of sexual sins and live a pure life, holy before our Lord. We can do it, but it starts with you. If you're a believer in Christ, you must give up pornography and sexual sins before Christ and begin today serving him in obedience. The Holy Spirit will help you stay true to God's values, but you need to surrender your

## Conclusion

will to Jesus. It is only by Christ that you can be saved. When you sin, you sin against the one who made you.

God is not an old man. Christ has his hands out, asking you to come to him. The weight of what I did is off my shoulders. Society wants me to always pay for what I did, but Christ paid for it on the cross. I don't have to carry the burden. Even when Satan tries to stop me from telling this story, I have the power from Christ to spread his message of hope for ALL. I will not be tricked by Satan. I will not pay attention to the liar and deceiver that he is. Christ alone can take this burden from you.

So, what is the answer again? It is Christ. No other source. He is the only living man who died on a cross, rose again, ascended to heaven, and sits on the throne in heaven right now making intercession for us. Name one person who has ever done that for us. There is none.

If you're a sex offender, God still loves you just as much as he would anyone else. Don't be fooled by Satan, thinking that God has forsaken you. If you're not a believer in Christ, then whose hands are guiding you? Who are you allowing to lead you through this world? It won't be Christ's hand if you have rejected him.

He will not force his creation to love him. So, who do you serve? Who is your master? Is your master the sin you're living in? Does it control your life? What hope do you have when you die? Unlike the believer in Christ, if you continue to live in sin, you will die lost in those sins. Every thought, every sinful action you made will be held against you. Are you certain of where your life is heading?

I have written this book for one reason—to tell many people how to be free from these sexual sins. Free from the addiction. I can tell you through my experience that living the life of sexual behaviors wore me out. I lost so much, and I have had to live with the pain of sin's consequences, things I can never get back.

Who are you now? Are you living your life all alone with no answers, no hope? Do you trust in your heavenly Father who will stop you, because he loves you too much for you to continue living disobedient to him?

The world's god is "self." It's always about self. For forty-four years, my life was about myself, my desires, my plans. God was determined to get my attention. I don't understand why he waited so long, but who am I to question God? I am to serve and listen to what he tells me. Do you want to be free from the burdens of life? You can give them to Christ. He has big shoulders. His heart is always open to the lost.

This story started out with the cost of pornography, but now I end it with this: There is hope through Jesus. Since the day I gave up pornography and all its trappings, life has been peaceful. Even though sometimes I wonder what God has in store for me next, I cling to the peace he has placed in my heart. Though this world is scary, I have the confidence that Christ will come and restore his earth when his plan will come to completion.

I ask you, what will you do with the rest of your life? Will you continue to ignore God and keep going in your own direction? Will you stop spending your time and money on the cost of pornography?

You have read my story of the cost of one look at a magazine. You can laugh and shrug your shoulders, but the ultimate question is, What will you do with Christ's offer of forgiveness? Will you reject him and go your separate way,

## Conclusion

or will you accept his forgiveness for the mess you made with your life? I chose to follow Christ. I hope you do too.

You are a sinner, separated from God. You must agree with God about that. You need to confess ALL your sins to him (1 John 1:9). He died on the cross for sins. Ask for forgiveness (Ephesians 2:8–9). You don't have to understand the whole Bible. Just know that you need to be forgiven and that you need God's help to change your life. Salvation is a gift from God, one that we don't deserve. He offers grace and mercy. Then, read the Bible every day.

The Gospel of John is good for new believers. If you repent from your heart, then Christ will forgive you. Your faith in Jesus will lead you to obey his Word. Your obedience to his Word will lead you to salvation where ALL your sins will be forgiven. That grace and mercy continues to transform me to be like Christ. With Christ, you always win. You can't lose!

I would be lying if I were to say that being a Christian is running through a field filled with roses and that your life will be perfect; it won't be. Being a believer in Christ is a process that God uses to draw you closer to him in fellowship. He teaches us how to trust in him.

How would you know how to trust in him if all were perfect? That hasn't come yet. The road to heaven is smooth, but the person on that road keeps running off and giving in to temptations that lure him, such as depraved sexual behaviors. They seem delightful, but they will cause you to suffer losses. If only we would stay on the straight and narrow road. But when we stray, the place on that smooth path is marked for you when you return. Then you continue that process of growing as a Christian.

It ends when you die or when Christ returns for us. Where on that path will you be marked? How much did you grow by walking and talking with Christ? Just picture you and Jesus walking one way on that path. Ahead of you is heaven with its bright shiny lights, but you can't enter until you die. That path is peaceful when you're on it, but when you walk away, that life is full of stress and depression, but you learn from it and trust the Lord to bring you back on that peaceful path.

When you fail, don't give up. When you fall into sexual temptations, instantly come back to the Father. He will always be there to welcome you back. But the thought of peace through Jesus gives us the true meaning of who he is.

## Final Words

It has taken me three years to write this book as correctly as I could. Now that you have come to the end of my journey, I ask you, "Is this you?" Are you going down that same path as I did? You might be in tears asking the same questions I did. It's hard to live an immoral life in secret. It's depressing. You question whether life is worth living. But if you are alive, God knows you have great value.

I could lie and say that treatment rescued me, or that my PO rescued me, or many others who lifted a hand, but that would only be half true. There are some things I can't explain, but I always knew the presence of the Holy Spirit was guiding me, and the hand of Christ was always picking me up. I don't know why he paid so much attention to me. But I know he will someday show me. There are some things the believer won't know until he gets to the other side of this life, which is in the presence of the King.

## Conclusion

God's power and his mercy overpower any of Satan's tricks. I know that God loves me so much. I know he saw all my tears. He saw my heart crying out. But I wouldn't be who I am today if it weren't for my heavenly Father. I have this compassion for people like I have never had before. The things I thought gave me pleasure were only temporary.

Each Christian goes through a process by the Holy Spirit to be like Jesus—not to be him, but to be like him. That's what I want. Why do I want to be like anything on this earth that one day will be burned up? Or who wants to follow the destructive power that Satan offers? How can we think of anything but the awe of God? We are without words or thoughts. I saw nothing but love from Christ. He understood every move I made.

How can anyone think that they can bargain with Christ when they stand before him, lost! God's love is also JUST. He must judge sin, and when you stand before him holding all your sins, what will you trade with him? You have a debt owed to God. How can you bargain with someone who owns the universe, when you messed it up by your disobedience?

You have nothing to bargain with God. You had all those chances to give away all your sins, but you waited to see what would happen. Gambling with your life will be the biggest mistake you will ever make.

**Don't do it.**
**Jesus loves me this I know. Why?**
**Because the Bible tells me so.**

## About the Author

Bob Gushwa served in the Army for almost 12 years in Germany and Italy. After leaving the service, he worked in transportation for 38 years, traveling throughout the US and Canada.

After having been raised in Indiana with a Christian background, he left it behind to fulfill what he thought would please him. Bad choices and painful consequences were made during those years.

This story is told in hopes that people will know the struggles that pornography causes.

www.ingramcontent.com/pod-product-compliance
Lightning Source LLC
Chambersburg PA
CBHW072000110526
44592CB00012B/1158